BARGAINING FOR
PEACE

BARGAINING FOR PEACE

South Africa and the National Peace Accord

Peter Gastrow

UNITED STATES
INSTITUTE OF PEACE PRESS
Washington, D.C.

The views expressed in this book are those of the author alone. They do not necessarily reflect views of the United States Institute of Peace.

United States Institute of Peace
1550 M Street, N.W.
Washington, D.C. 20005

First published 1995

Printed in the United States of America

The paper used in this publication meets the minimum requirements of American National Standard for Information Sciences—Permanence of Paper for Printed Library Materials, ANSI Z39.48-1984.

Library of Congress Cataloging-in-Publication Data
Gastrow, Peter, 1947–
    South Africa : political violence and the National Peace Accord / Peter Gastrow.
      p.   cm.
    Includes bibliographical references and index.
    ISBN 1-878379-40-2 (alk. paper). — ISBN 1-878379-39-9 (pbk. : alk. paper)
      1. South Africa—Politics and government—1989– 2. Violence—South Africa.
3. National Peace Accord (1991 : South Africa)
I. Title.
DT1970.G37 1994
968.06'4—dc20   94-28463
                                                      CIP

CONTENTS

Figures

PREFACE

The term "negotiated revolution" is an apt description of the rapid and tumultuous changes taking place in South Africa since 1990.[1] Revolutions always seem impossible before they happen and inevitable afterward. The same is likely to be true of South Africa's rapid transition from apartheid to a new democracy unless we constantly remind ourselves of the uniqueness of the recent developments.

Much of what has occurred during the past several years is nothing short of miraculous and should not be taken for granted. As happens with revolutions, the changes in South Africa were triggered by the vision and determined actions of many individuals as well as by national and international developments. There was nothing inevitable about them. To write about these events while the status quo ante is still fresh in the mind, and while the process of change remains quite brittle and far from complete, is one way of ensuring that recent developments are not taken for granted. A proper historical perspective will be lacking, but that can be added by others in the future.

One of the products of the political transition in South Africa is the National Peace Accord (NPA) and its structures—something that would have been unimaginable a few years ago. Signed by the leaders of all major political parties in September 1991, the NPA is an extraordinary and daring experiment in conflict resolution on a national scale. It was aimed at addressing the endemic political violence and rampant political intolerance in the country. It had become essential for political leaders to jointly address these issues, as political violence was increasingly preventing multiparty constitutional negotiations from commencing.

The NPA is in fact without precedent internationally. Special forums have been established elsewhere in the world to settle disputes peacefully, but nowhere has this been done through a countrywide network of peace committees at the local, regional, and national levels, operating with the formal mandate of government and major political parties.

This book constitutes an attempt by a practitioner who was involved in some of the events that created the NPA, and who serves on the National Peace Committee and the National Peace Secretariat, to provide an account of the initiatives and events that led to the signing of the NPA. Some reference is made to the content of the accord and to its implementation through the establishment of a countrywide network of peace structures.

This volume also tries to address the question, Has it worked? In doing so, the book examines the NPA's effect on political violence, on the democratization process, and on socioeconomic reconstruction and development. While some of the strengths and weaknesses of the NPA are examined, this book does not attempt to evaluate these strengths and weaknesses in detail. That has been done by others far better placed to do so. The most recent critical evaluation is contained in a report prepared by an international evaluation mission cosponsored by the National Peace Secretariat and International Alert, an alliance of several nongovernmental organizations based in London.

A comparative study of other plural, violence-ridden societies in transition would have significantly enriched this contribution. So would an analysis of existing conflict resolution models and theories and their relevance to the South African conflicts. The limited time I had available for this project prevented me from venturing into these areas.

In writing this book, I have drawn on my own experience as an participant in some of the events, as well as interviews I conducted and research I did in primary and secondary sources that are cited in the notes.

I am grateful to the United States Institute of Peace for awarding me a Visiting Fellowship. It enabled me to extract myself from the intensity of daily events in South Africa and spend time in a much calmer Washington, D.C., to pursue this project. The staff of the Institute and other fellows from different parts of the world were always ready to assist, for which I thank them.

Because of the author's time restrictions, the main text of this book sketches the developments in South Africa only until the end of September 1993. The crucial seven-month period leading up to the first democratic elections, in April 1994, was therefore not dealt with. A brief epilogue has since been added to cover that historic period. This book therefore spans the period of South Africa's transition for which the NPA was primarily designed. A new phase for all peace structures has started since the elections. A debate is presently under way to determine their future role in the new South Africa.

ABBREVIATIONS

ANC	African National Congress
AZAPO	Azanian People's Organization
CBM	Consultative Business Movement
CODESA	Convention for a Democratic South Africa
COSATU	Congress of South African Trade Unions
EC	European Community
IEC	Independent Electoral Commission
IFP	Inkatha Freedom Party
LDRC	Local dispute resolution committee (later known as local peace committee)
LPC	Local peace committee
NPA	National Peace Accord
NPC	National Peace Committee
NPS	National Peace Secretariat
OAU	Organization of African Unity
PAC	Pan-Africanist Congress
PWV	Pretoria-Witwatersrand-Vereeniging
RDRC	Regional dispute resolution committee (later known as regional peace committee)
RPC	Regional peace committee
SACC	South African Council of Churches
SACCOLA	South African Consultative Committee on Labour Affairs
SACOB	South African Chamber of Business
TEC	Transitional Executive Council

BARGAINING FOR
PEACE

INTRODUCTION

Violent political conflict has been part of South African history for centuries. When the first European settlers arrived in Cape Town in the mid-seventeenth century, a conflict that had been part of the existence of the indigenous groups—namely, the struggle for control over land—took on a new dimension because of the settlers' superior firearms and their completely different understanding of the concepts of ownership and control of land. Early colonial settlers met with resistance from indigenous inhabitants. The Boers, who were farmers of Dutch, German, and French origin, trekked into the interior in search of grazing land for cattle and to escape Dutch and British colonial rule. They encountered ongoing resistance from indigenous tribes such as the Xhosa and Zulu, resulting in fierce battles of subjugation. British imperial designs on the two independent Boer republics established in the interior—the Transvaal and the Orange Free State—led to Afrikaner resistance and culminated in the South African War of 1899 to 1902 (also called the Boer War).

The 1910 constitution of the Union of South Africa was premised on white supremacy and provided the stepping-stones for the implementation of apartheid soon after the Afrikaner-based National Party won the general election in 1948. Resistance from the black population against white minority rule changed from weak and tentative at the beginning of this century to intense but mainly nonviolent in the 1950s. Violent state oppression and popular resistance and revolt reached unprecedented levels during the 1970s and 1980s. The white minority government responded with coercive security measures in its effort to cling to power, while the antiapartheid struggle changed its focus from political protest to popular insurrection and the "armed struggle." By 1989, a political and strategic deadlock between the state and the antiapartheid forces had developed. The government controlled substantial resources and had its hands on the levers of power, but it had little public support or legitimacy and was isolated internationally. On the other hand, the leading opponent of apartheid, the African National Congress (ANC), was still banned, had meager resources, and was unable to get its hands on the levers of state power, but it enjoyed broad legitimacy, public support, and wide international recognition and support. It became clear to the government that its coercive security option would not provide lasting solutions, and the ANC realized that its armed struggle was incapable of delivering victory.

Nelson Mandela had begun, from 1986 onward, to prepare the ground for possible negotiations, something that at that stage must have seemed a remote possibility. From prison he began corresponding with key players outside, including President F. W. de Klerk's predecessor, P. W. Botha. Secret meetings were held with cabinet ministers such as Justice Minister Kobie Coetzee.

A breakthrough came on February 2, 1990, when President de Klerk made his now-famous speech during the opening of the South African Parliament. This was the month that saw South Africa extricating itself from the political cul de sac into which apartheid had led it. The political and strategic deadlock was broken when de Klerk announced the unbanning of political organizations, the release of political leaders from prison, and free political activity for all. When, a few days after these announcements, Mandela left prison a free man after twenty-seven years of incarceration, South Africans from all walks of life felt great optimism. He received a tumultuous welcome from supporters in Cape Town. In Natal, the province in which Chief Minister Mangosuthu Buthelezi has his power base, Mandela addressed a rally in Durban shortly after his release, attended by an estimated 100,000 people.

Business leaders hailed President de Klerk's February speech, predicting that it would lead to improved foreign perceptions of South Africa and ease pressure for further economic sanctions against the country. The dramatic political events provided a welcome justification for South Africans to move their focus away from the debilitating political violence of the previous year. Measured in fatalities, 1989 had been the worst year of political violence in modern South African history. A total of 1,403 persons had been killed. Good news about South Africa was what both South Africans and the world wished for. Preliminary negotiations between the white government, led by the National Party, and the ANC, South Africa's largest and oldest liberation movement, provided reason to believe that proper multiparty constitutional negotiations were not far off.[2] The sudden real prospects for a negotiated settlement and the hope that political violence would abate instilled a sense of optimism and hope.

Violence did not abate, and some of the hope that had been generated was shown to have been misplaced. In fact, the year that many thought would be the precursor to liberation, democracy, and stability became a year of unprecedented political strife and violence: 1990 replaced 1989 as the worst year of political violence in modern South African history, with 3,699 persons killed (a 163 percent increase over 1989).[3]

1

VIOLENCE DURING POLITICAL TRANSITION

A Society Prone to Violence

Statistics on political violence over the past decade certainly suggest that South Africa is prone to violence.[4] Anthony Mathews provides two main reasons for this.[5] The first is that South Africa is a deeply divided society, characterized by significant racial, religious, ethnic, and linguistic divisions. Such societies are notorious for their political instability. Unlike discontented individuals who do not share a common identity, groups with a specific identity and a common set of grievances can mobilize support by appealing to those who identify with them culturally and racially.

The second characteristic of South African society that makes it more susceptible to instability and violent conflict is the modernization process to which its peoples have been subjected for several decades and which is likely to continue for a few more. Mathews describes the essential features of modernization as "rapid economic growth and the absorption of the masses into a modern economy accompanied by disruption of the traditional patterns of life, by urbanization and by large jumps in literacy, education and media exposure."[6] Modernization heightens the potential for disruption and violence in a deeply divided society because the many people who relocate to the more developed urban areas experience a new awareness of improved forms of life. They become aware of their relative deprivation. Traditional values, family life, and social institutions are disrupted and lose their binding influence. In

South Africa modernization and urbanization during the past decade have affected mainly the black population. In 1980 only about 33 percent of blacks lived in urban areas, while for whites and Asians the figure was close to 90 percent. According to the Urban Foundation, black urbanization had increased to 58 percent in 1992.[7] Much of this increase is reflected in the growth of informal settlements or shack dwellings.

A plural society undergoing modernization is therefore particularly prone to violence. It produces a powder keg whose ignition can only be prevented by great political skill. Added to this already explosive combination is a third reason South Africa is prone to violence: the political transition it is presently undergoing. The transition has created increased expectations for most South Africans, greater fear and anxiety for minorities, and growing rivalry among political groups. The increased political competition has tended to feed on ethnic, racial, and class differences, thereby increasing polarization in an already deeply divided society.

The combined consequences of deep divisions, modernization, and transition therefore pose an ongoing threat to South Africa's stability. Political leaders face the challenge of finding political solutions to neutralize the tensions that inevitably arise from such a combination of factors. The security responses of the past have failed to address the underlying causes of the tensions in South African society. A political response is what is required. Mathews argues that the instability inherent in a socially pluralistic society needs to be addressed through the introduction of constitutional mechanisms designed to reduce intergroup conflict and maximize intergroup cooperation.[8] The conflict produced by modernization needs to be anticipated and defused through deliberate political programs to incorporate the newly mobilized groups into political decision making at all levels. These are matters that form part of the negotiations for a new constitution for South Africa. Present indications are that, once finalized, the new constitution will go much further than previous constitutions in accommodating the needs of the country's pluralistic society.

The political response that the South African government devised in the early 1980s to deal with the growing demand for equal political rights was the opposite of what it should have been. The 1983 tricameral constitution, aimed at "broadening democracy," included participation by Indians and coloreds but expressly excluded black South Africans from political participation—the very group that has been most intensely affected by modernization. In 1991 blacks constituted 74.8 percent of the total population, whites 14.1 percent, Indians 2.6 percent, and coloreds 8.5 percent.[9] The nationwide protest that the introduction of that constitution elicited resulted in the growing revolt against the government during the 1980s. This was the period during which political violence became a permanent feature of South African political life. Between 1985 and 1989 a total of 5,387 persons died as a result of political violence.[10]

After the February 1990 speech by de Klerk, the new challenge to all political leaders was to manage the coming transition and to minimize violence during a period when the planned political and constitutional reforms were not yet in place. The response of South Africa's political leaders was to seek agreement among each other about the norms and standards of political and police conduct that would apply during the period of transition. The National Peace Accord (NPA) eventually came into being to meet this need.

The violence of the past few years of transition should therefore be seen against the background of an abandonment of the failed coercive security responses of the past, the absence of new political or constitutional responses (which were still to be finalized through negotiations), a competitive transition resulting in intensified political rivalry, and growing polarization. Add to these factors a deep economic recession that contributed to a massive rise in unemployment and widespread poverty, and the complexity of the factors involved in political violence becomes apparent.

The term "political violence" has been used very loosely in South Africa. Reliance on the word "political" to distinguish it from other forms of violence, such as criminal violence, inevitably blurs such distinctions because of the difficulty in providing a neat definition of "political." Political violence, criminal violence, police violence, "third force" violence, and community violence are all concepts that can overlap. Case studies into the activities of some of the more prominent criminal gangs and "self-defense units" established in some black townships after February 1990 show that the dividing lines between political and criminal violence, for example, are in many cases artificial.[11] What starts out as political violence often becomes criminal and vice versa. In many cases there is a straightforward and cynical exploitation of political violence by criminals for their own benefit. Defining "political violence" is therefore problematic.

Graeme Simpson and others have based their definition on the sub-
jective criterion of motive. They argue that political violence is "that violence which occurs between individuals or groups where the dominant
motivation is based on political difference or the competing desire for
political power."[12] André Du Toit provides a somewhat broader definition: "Political violence is typically differentiated from other forms of
violence by claims to a special moral or public legitimation for the
injury and harm done to others."[13] To provide a watertight definition
that does not overlap with personal or other forms of violence, or with
legitimated violence by agents of the state, is not possible. A further
variation on the definitions provided above is even broader, but it is the
one I prefer to adopt for the purpose of this book. It defines political
violence as "violent behavior which is intended in some way to influence the political process."[14] It is comprehensive and flexible but clearly
not definitive enough to exclude overlaps.

Deescalation/Escalation of Political Violence

The inability of the major players to curtail the political violence
brought home the complexity of its underlying causes. During the
1970s and 1980s the problem was not as complex, since political violence was usually a logical consequence of political conditions existing
at the time. South Africa's disenfranchised, mainly blacks, were in revolt
against the white minority government and its agents.

The political transition toward a nonracial democracy, which commenced in earnest with President de Klerk's February 1990 speech and
the unbanning of organizations, saw a dramatic change in the nature of
the violence. No longer were the state and its agents the prime targets.
Du Toit points out that the trends and patterns of conflict that emerged
from this transition showed strong paradoxical features: "The transition
has involved both a significant turn from political violence as well as a
marked escalation of political violence."[15]

What occurred during the transition was that at the formal level, the
mainly black-supported liberation movement—the ANC and its allies—
turned from the politics of violence to the politics of negotiation. Popular insurrection, armed struggle, and the international sanctions of the
1980s were replaced by an essentially nonviolent attempt to reach a
new constitutional order through negotiated settlement. At another
level, the transition was marked by an increase in what appeared to be

endemic political violence in many black townships and some rural areas of Natal. In the mid-1970s, political violence killed an average of 44 persons per month. In the middle and late 1980s the monthly average had risen to 86, and in the 1990s it was more than 250.[16] Most of the deaths in the 1970s and early 1980s were caused by the police, but in the late 1980s and the 1990s a growing proportion resulted from black factional violence.

Attempts by South African researchers and commentators to identify the root causes of political violence in townships often resulted in controversy, finger-pointing, apportioning of blame, and inevitable counter-accusations. Political agendas have often been served by blaming opposing political groups for the violence. The de Klerk regime and its security forces, the communists and insurrectionists within the ANC, and the warlords and hostel dwellers of Inkatha have all been said to be responsible. Unemployment, poverty, and social disruption have been put forward as the major contributing factors. Others have tended to attribute the violence to rivalries originating from ethnic differences. Generalizations that suggest the violence is the result of two ethnic groups—the Xhosa and the Zulu—fighting for dominance are common. Some took the easy way out, either by blaming all the violence on apartheid or by describing it as simply a "black-on-black" fight between the ANC and Inkatha. It has frequently been suggested that the violence is being fueled by a "third force," sponsored by the state or consisting of disaffected right-wing elements with links to the security forces.

The many single-cause explanations for the violence have, to say the least, not made it any easier to identify solutions. The irony is that many of these reasons contain elements of truth that, if linked with others, provide partial explanations for the causes of political violence. It has been correctly stated that "probably no other aspect of the South African conflict has elicited more divergent explanations and misinterpretations than the ongoing political violence. A credible comprehensive account of the violence has yet to be produced, despite dozens of articles and books on the topic."[17]

The reality is that from 1990, the year in which the "normalization" of political activities commenced, until the end of September 1993, a total of 10,495 died as a result of political violence. Until the middle of 1990 the violence was largely confined to the province of Natal. Opinion makers, the media, and the government regarded it as a regional matter that required local solutions. Because the media did not accord it the national prominence it deserved, the public at large was not as well informed about the gravity of the violence as it could have been. Predominantly white residential areas were not affected. The violence occurred mainly in periurban shack settlements and townships where blacks were living under squalid conditions with inadequate facilities. The so-called Natal violence had a distinctly political flavor, as it was shaped by clashes between ANC-supporting youth and Inkatha supporters. In some instances, the roles of the KwaZulu Police and the South African Police were contributing factors. They often displayed a clear bias toward Inkatha and as a result became a source of additional tension by their presence in conflict situations.[18] The conflict between the warring factions was a struggle for power and control of territory, structures, and resources. It was characterized by indiscriminate massacres (incidents in which more than five persons were killed), large-scale intimidation, and preemptive and retaliatory attacks by armed supporters on each other. Lack of political tolerance marked the conflict. Inkatha has estimated that in Natal alone fifty so-called no-go areas existed, where ANC supporters had established a hegemony and Inkatha supporters were either driven out or prevented from conducting politics openly.[19] Similar no-go areas controlled by Inkatha existed in many parts, particularly in the self-governing territory of KwaZulu. Mistrust of the security forces, and a lack of faith in the legal process, contributed to a general breakdown in law and order in violence-ridden areas. Perpetrators were not being apprehended or successfully prosecuted. Lack of trust in the system as well as widespread intimidation resulted in witnesses refusing to come forward to testify in court.

Until March 1990 the most common form of conflict in Natal had been small-scale attacks on people and property. This pattern changed when between March 25 and 31, 1991, Inkatha launched large-scale attacks on ANC-supporting townships near Pietermaritzburg in Natal. During these attacks and counterattacks, about 130 persons were killed in what became known as the Seven Days' War.[20] Hundreds were injured, many houses were destroyed, and thousands became refugees.[21]

Large-scale violence spread to the Johannesburg area in July 1990 with the first such outbreak between ANC and Inkatha supporters occurring at Sebokeng, a township near Johannesburg, on July 22. Twenty-seven persons died in that encounter. Inkatha was determined to gain a foothold in the Transvaal, while ANC supporters were determined to keep them out. Supporters of political groups other than the ANC and

Inkatha were also victims of the reigning political intolerance and the urge to establish political hegemony. In October 1990, a mass funeral organized by the Pan-Africanist Congress (PAC) in Kagiso, near Krugersdorp in the Transvaal, was disrupted by knife-wielding ANC and Communist Party supporters, who shouted down the speakers and tore down banners.

A Helpless Leadership

In the Transvaal the conflict often acquired an ethnic dimension. Inkatha had strong support from many of the Zulu residents of the single-men hostels who had moved to the Transvaal to seek work. When conflict and violence arose between hostel dwellers and the surrounding communities, the hostels were often labeled by the communities as Zulu and Inkatha strongholds. Inkatha leaders fueled ethnic tensions by repeatedly referring to the ANC as Xhosa-dominated and anti-Zulu.

As the number of deaths resulting from political violence continued to rise during 1990, desperation set in among political and church leaders. The business sector predicted a delay in the lifting of sanctions and in the negotiating process unless political violence was checked. The ANC, which was struggling to find its feet after decades of being banned, underground, and in exile, experienced the violence as debilitating and undermining of its attempts to establish grassroots structures. President de Klerk and his ruling National Party were embarrassed by their apparent inability to contain the violence, which weakened their negotiating power and played into the hands of a growing white right wing. Chief Minister Buthelezi and Inkatha were subjected to growing local and international criticism for the open involvement of Inkatha supporters in the Natal and Transvaal violence.

By the end of 1990 it had become clear that political violence was directly undermining every relevant political group in the country. It was retarding progress toward constitutional negotiations, and South Africa's longer-term stability was under a growing threat. This threat, and consequently what to do about the violence, became the most important point for discussion at bilateral meetings between de Klerk and Mandela. In a joint press statement issued after the two met on December 8, 1990, they confirmed that "our main concern was the ongoing violence."[22] Three days later, newspapers were carrying headlines such as "100 dead in 8 days of unrest on east and west rand."[23]

Meetings by the country's senior political leaders had no effect at the grassroots level, and calls by church leaders to end the violence were ignored. The year 1990 had been a gloomy one for South Africa as far as political violence was concerned.

The start of 1991 produced a fleeting ray of hope. Led by Mandela and Buthelezi, respectively—the ANC and Inkatha, now transformed into the Inkatha Freedom Party (IFP)[24]—met in January to thrash out what was at the time described as a "watershed agreement effectively outlawing violence, intimidation and political intolerance among their followers."[25] One day later, a fierce battle between more than 2,000 supporters of the ANC and the IFP took place at Umgababa in Natal. At least 8 persons were killed, 60 injured, and about 56 houses burned to the ground.[26] During March alone, 314 persons lost their lives.[27] The impression gained ground among church and business leaders that violence was out of control and that neither the political leadership nor the security forces were able to address it effectively. The South African Council of Churches (SACC) issued a statement describing political leaders as impotent to stop the violence: "Either the parties involved in the crises have failed, or the violence has now simply gone beyond the control of the organizations themselves."[28]

Yet eight months later, on September 14, 1991, the NPA was signed by political and labor leaders across the national spectrum. The signing of this unique document signified a breakthrough that enabled the diverse political leadership in South Africa to meet in the same room for the first time to pursue a common objective. The events, pressures, and influences that shaped the process leading to the signing of the National Peace Accord have not yet been recorded. They provide a case study of how, despite deep divisions within a plural and multiethnic society, and despite a history of conflict, violence, and oppression, a convergence of interests can lead to a pact among the political leadership to make peace and to jointly move toward democracy.

2

SHAPING THE
NATIONAL
PEACE
ACCORD

Church Interventions

At the beginning of 1991, the church was the institution that first attempted a national intervention in what seemed to be a scenario of worsening political violence and instability. In March, the SACC said in a statement that in its view there was an urgent need for the church to intervene in an attempt to stop the violence that was escalating despite peace talks between rival political parties. As its contribution to efforts aimed at ending factional violence in the country, the SACC planned to convene an urgent national meeting of all leaders of strife-torn communities within a week. While the SACC did not include all the churches in South Africa, it issued the statement at a time when the country's churches as a whole were closer to each other on the issue of violence than they had been for many decades. Before 1990, deep theological and political differences among churches kept them from taking a united stand on many important social and political issues. Between 70 and 80 percent of South Africans profess to be Christians. The potential influence of the churches, if they could act together, was therefore not to be underestimated.

During the previous six decades, Afrikaner churches had provided theological justification for apartheid until, in 1986, they rejected apartheid and finally, in 1990, declared it a sin. During the apartheid years, deep differences existed between the Afrikaner churches and those represented by the SACC, such as the Methodist and Anglican

Churches. The latter had been strong critics of apartheid. The saying that South Africa was one of the most Christian but also one of the most divided countries in the world was not without foundation.

Significant strides toward unity were made at a major national church conference held at the town of Rustenburg, in the central Transvaal, during November 1990. All churches and Christian religious groups in South Africa were invited. Only two, both white right-wing churches, refused the invitation.[29] The 300 participants represented some 80 denominations and 40 religious organizations. The conference was historic in that the major Afrikaner church, the Dutch Reformed Church (Nederduitse Gereformeerde Kerk), publicly confessed guilt in regard to apartheid and its own involvement and participation in a system of discrimination. This confession led to a mood of reconciliation that was reflected in the statement issued by the conference, entitled the Rustenburg Declaration. The declaration denounced apartheid, called for a democratic constitution and a more equitable distribution of wealth, and urged churches to condemn all forms of violence. Among the many other provisions of the Rustenburg Declaration was a commitment to establish a committee that would coordinate church strategies and organize a peace conference to bring together leaders who could assist in ending violence. The committee was set up by the conference to facilitate communication between the churches and to encourage them to support the implementation of the Rustenburg Declaration. It was headed by the Reverend Frank Chikane, general secretary of the SACC, and Louw Alberts, a lay church person with considerable interdenominational experience and direct access to the mainly white Afrikaner power establishment. Alberts was a scientist and past chairman of the Atomic Energy Board. Both Chikane and Alberts later played key roles in the peace process. For the first time in decades, the churches were collectively addressing key sociopolitical issues in South Africa.

At the same time that the SACC was calling for a church intervention, Archbishop Desmond Tutu of Cape Town, a Nobel Peace Prize winner, made a passionate appeal to black politicians for renewed realism in their fight against violence.[30] This happened a few days before Mandela and Buthelezi met for an "Easter crisis summit." The calls from the churches did not seem to affect either side at the meeting. Buthelezi subsequently launched an attack on "naive" churchmen, referring specifically to Chikane. The call for peace by some churchmen, he said, "unfortunately suggests that leading churchmen are actually busybodies

trying to be important in the eyes of the world by stepping in and trying to take charge of the peace process."[31]

Buthelezi had for many years regarded the SACC as being close and
sympathetic to the ANC and its supporting organizations. His attack on
Chikane and others was therefore nothing new. More important, it was
a clear message to the churches that not all political groups found them
acceptable as facilitators in the peace process. It raised the concomitant
question, If the churches were not acceptable facilitators, who else
would be? Who else would be able to bring together opposing political
groupings such as the governing National Party, the PAC, the ANC, and
the IFP to get them to jointly address the issue of political violence?

While the SACC's bold offer to call a peace conference within a week
was an indication of the urgency with which it viewed the problem, it
also showed a lack of preparation and an underestimation of the complexity of the issues. The plans for a peace conference during March
1991 were not taken further, since it was apparent that little would be
achieved in the absence of key players, such as the IFP.

Role of Business

Another interest group, the Consultative Business Movement (CBM),
consisting of the more progressive elements of the business sector, was
also exploring ways to deal with the ongoing political violence during
this period. CBM is a voluntary organization of senior South African business leaders who acknowledged and supported the need for a constructive transformation of the country's political economy.[32] The much larger
and more representative umbrella organization representing commerce
and industry nationwide, the South African Chamber of Business
(SACOB), appears not to have been involved. SACOB was more conventional in its approach, focusing on the narrower interests of the business establishment. It tended to steer a safe course that would avoid
controversy from either the government or its membership. CBM had
approximately ninety corporate members, very few compared with the
membership of SACOB, but representing the largest mining, publish-
ing, manufacturing, and chemical concerns in the country, among others.
Its activities were primarily driven by a dynamic full-time staff operating
from the Johannesburg head office. The executive director was Dr. Theuns
Eloff, a young former minister of religion in one of the smaller Afrikaner
churches, who fell into disfavor with his church after attending a meeting

in Dakar, Senegal, in 1987 at which a group of mainly Afrikaner intellectuals engaged the then-banned ANC for the first time.

During 1990, CBM had concluded that the violence was destructive to the negotiation process, the economy, and people's personal lives and that it ought to investigate the violence to formulate an informed response from business leaders. CBM foresaw the possibility that it would act as a facilitator and proceeded with a lengthy process of consultations with political and labor groups and individuals who were either involved in or relevant to the political violence.

By March 1991, CBM had prepared a memorandum on the violence, focusing mainly on the Pretoria-Witwatersrand-Vereeniging (PWV) area in the Transvaal. By this time political violence had moved to the top of the country's agenda, and as business was also viewing the violence as a major concern, CBM decided that its memorandum and its concerns should be taken directly to the major players. Low-key meetings were held with a delegation of senior cabinet ministers in Cape Town on March 26, 1991, and with the National Violence Committee of the ANC alliance in Johannesburg on March 27. Also present were representatives from the two alliance partners, the South African Communist Party and the largest labor union federation in the country, the Congress of South African Trade Unions (COSATU). A third meeting took place a few weeks later with Chief Minister Buthelezi and the Central Executive Committee of the IFP on May 7, 1991. Nothing concrete emerged from these meetings, but CBM had placed itself on the map as an organization deeply concerned about the violence and prepared to play a facilitating role in dealing with it.

The political temperature in the country rose further when, on April 5, 1991, the ANC announced that unless the de Klerk government met a seven-point ultimatum before May 9, it would call off talks with the government about an all-party conference and the negotiations on a new constitution. At a press conference, Mandela blamed the government and security force inaction or complicity for the thousands of deaths in the factional strife of the past few years. Among other demands, the ANC called for the dismissal of the minister of defense and the minister of law and order, a ban on the public display of all weapons, and the suspension of certain policemen who had been involved in shootings in townships around Johannesburg. These steps, the ANC believed, would contribute significantly toward reducing violence. The spotlight was now on President de Klerk to see whether and how he would respond. It had become clear to all that political violence could wreck the chances of constitutional negotiations unless an effective intervention took place.

In Parliament, the Democratic Party urged President de Klerk to intervene decisively by calling a peace summit of leaders reflecting all interests and sections in South Africa. A day later, Law and Order Minister Adriaan Vlok announced that the government intended to call a multiparty conference of all organizations to decide how to combat violence.[33] A day after Vlok's announcement, a meeting planned earlier took place between the ANC National Executive Committee and a Rustenburg Conference delegation of church leaders. Under the leadership of Chikane and Alberts, the church delegation briefed the ANC about the Rustenburg Declaration and listened to an ANC presentation on the violence. At the end of the meeting, ANC deputy president Mandela rejected Vlok's call for a multiparty conference. He told a press conference that it was a "propaganda ploy" in preparation for President de Klerk's visit to Europe.[34]

President de Klerk's Peace Summit

On April 18, President de Klerk announced that he would convene a two-day summit on violence to be held in Pretoria on May 24 and 25.[35] Political, church, and community leaders would be invited to discuss violence and intimidation. The IFP welcomed the initiative. So did parliamentary parties, with the exception of the white right-wing Conservative Party, which said it would not take part in any discussions with the ANC, the Communist Party, or other "perpetrators of violence."[36] While these various pronouncements were being made and debated, political violence was continuing to take its toll in many townships. During the last weekend of April alone, 50 persons were reported killed in Natal and on the Witwatersrand (the area around Johannesburg), with close to 200 wounded.[37]

Opposition to de Klerk's planned peace summit was more widespread than many had anticipated. At May Day rallies throughout the country, leaders of COSATU, as well as ANC leaders, reiterated their rejection of the government's peace summit. Speakers described de Klerk as partisan on the issue of violence and said that he should not have called such a summit. They argued that such a summit should be convened by an independent party. The ANC viewed national initiatives undertaken unilaterally by de Klerk with great caution and suspicion. He was, after all, their main political opponent. The ANC was especially suspicious of the planned peace summit, regarding it as inappropriate for de Klerk, as one of those responsible for political violence, to convene and host such an important event. Many outside the ANC found it difficult to understand its reasoning. Some regarded the ANC's stand as unreasonable and actively mobilized public support for the peace summit. Organized commerce and industry, for example, called for nationwide support of de Klerk's summit in a statement and a prominent press advertisement placed by SACOB.[38] President de Klerk argued that he felt compelled to call the summit because he and the government bore the ultimate responsibility for maintaining law and order. He asked the ANC to reconsider its position.

May 9, the deadline for the ultimatum that the ANC had issued on April 5, was rapidly approaching. Public anxiety grew as it became absolutely clear that President de Klerk had no intention of meeting all the conditions. A delegation of senior church leaders, spurred by the specter of another deadlock looming, embarked on low-key confidential meetings with both Mandela and de Klerk, hoping to avoid a serious confrontation between the parties and to discuss the political violence in the country.[39] A last-minute meeting between de Klerk and Buthelezi, during which a compromise deal on traditional weapons was thrashed out, was held just hours before the ultimatum was to expire.

To the relief of many, none of the major political parties made an issue of the ultimatum after May 9. Shuttle diplomacy involving church, political, and business leaders appeared to have won the day. But the political violence remained an issue. So did the peace summit called by President de Klerk. It was clear that the summit would take place on May 24 and 25, and it was equally clear that important players such as the ANC, COSATU, and the PAC would not attend. Holding the summit without these players might exacerbate tensions and divisions and lead to a worsening of violence. Chikane, general secretary of the SACC, announced on the day the ultimatum expired that church leaders were planning a national peace conference if all parties did not attend President de Klerk's peace summit later in the month. He said a conference of "affected communities" would not include the government and that an attempt would be made to establish a code of conduct and violence-monitoring mechanisms. "We hope that out of that we will engage government," Chikane said.[40] Church leaders would travel to Ulundi, the administrative capital of the self-governing territory of KwaZulu, to meet with Buthelezi to persuade him to take part in the conference.

Mandela welcomed the peace conference proposed by the SACC when he addressed 107 of South Africa's most prominent businessmen in Johannesburg on May 16.[41] At the meeting, held under the auspices of the CBM, he explained why the ANC would not attend de Klerk's peace summit, scheduled for eight days later, on May 24 and 25. He appealed to de Klerk not to go ahead with the summit. The response from the businessmen was mixed. They were not persuaded to pressure de Klerk to cancel the peace summit. "ANC briefing disappoints businessmen" was a headline in the Johannesburg daily, the *Business Day*. Mandela also used the opportunity to urge the businessmen to help end political violence.

CBM immediately took this challenge up and decided at an emergency meeting held the next morning, May 17, that the critical situation in the country made it necessary for the business community (CBM and SACOB) and the churches to jointly explore how to keep the negotiation process on track.[42] The national organizer of CBM, Colin Coleman, met with Chikane on the same day and raised this issue. He learned from Chikane that the SACC proposal for a peace conference had been received poorly by Buthelezi in Ulundi. Buthelezi had publicly labeled the churches as partisan.[43] The church initiative, as envisaged by the SACC, was therefore unlikely to succeed.

Coleman and Chikane considered what to do about de Klerk's peace summit, which many saw as a potentially polarizing event. Danger signs were clearly visible. Business had been disappointed by Mandela. The ANC was therefore unlikely to entrust organized business with the role of facilitator. Business was clearly not positioned to resolve the issue. The churches had been labeled as partisan and would therefore not be able to bring all relevant parties together. Something had to be done to ensure that the 1990 political initiative was pursued to its ultimate conclusion of a democratic South Africa. Coleman and Chikane were concerned about indications that pre-1990 lines of division and polarization were reappearing. They felt that both the churches and organized business, being part of civil society and nonpartisan, had an obligation to stem such a development. Some of the post-1990 alliances or relationships between organizations and individuals that developed on a nonpartisan basis were being threatened by the planned peace summit, the violence, and people's response to these events. At the grassroots level, the leadership of many of the mainly black churches was being pressured by their members to adopt stronger stances against de Klerk and the IFP.

Such positions moved those churches and the SACC closer to the ANC, as they had been during the 1980s and before. The business sector—which since 1990 had attempted to remain independent of the ANC, the governing National Party, and the IFP—was now publicly promoting de Klerk's peace summit.

Coleman and Chikane raised the possibility of the churches and organized business joining forces, perhaps with other nonpartisan groups from civil society—or at least from relatively uninvolved groups—to bring all the parties together. Their conclusion was to proceed immediately, and a meeting, hosted jointly by the SACC and CBM, was called as a matter of urgency for later that same afternoon. Present at that meeting were representatives from the SACC, CBM, and SACOB, including the then president of SACOB, John Hall, who would later become the chairperson of the National Peace Committee. Jay Naidoo, secretary-general of COSATU and a person with direct access to the National Executive Committee of the ANC (with which COSATU was in alliance), was also asked to attend. So was a representative from the South African Consultative Committee on Labour Affairs (SACCOLA), a body representing employers in commerce and industry. For the first time ever, church, business, and trade union leaders were putting their heads together, albeit informally, to seek an answer to the problem of political violence and the pending peace summit. Should attempts be made to salvage the state president's summit, and if so, how should attendance by those political groups that had indicated that they would not be there be secured? Naidoo suggested that the ANC might consider attending the peace summit if de Klerk would agree to an independent chairman for the plenary sessions and if an agenda committee, with representatives of all participating parties, were established.[44] It was agreed to pursue this possibility by immediately faxing and telephoning the suggestion to the state president's office in Cape Town. A response from the state president's office was received the next morning on May 18. The president intended to proceed with the summit but agreed to make the point that the summit was part of an ongoing process and that he would ask a facilitating committee to bring all the parties together for another conference. He had no objection to the idea of an agenda committee and proposed that an independent agenda committee should meet within three days to discuss the proposed independent chairman for the peace summit.

The option of attending the peace summit subject to the procedures agreed to by de Klerk was considered by the ANC Executive Committee when it met that same day. The Executive Committee turned it down and reiterated its earlier decision not to attend.[45] What the committee did support was the idea, agreed to by de Klerk, that the peace summit should be part of a process and that a further peace conference should be held. It also supported the notion of an independently convened peace conference, involving all parties and organizations, which "needs to be a conference that reaches multi-lateral binding agreements with obligations on all parties to act in accordance with these agreements."[46]

All was not lost. The possibilities for a compromise were there, but it was essential to act with speed to ensure that the peace summit, although not attended by some key players, did not become too divisive. The danger was that it would be seen as the start of an exclusive process. A statement issued by the minister of constitutional development, Gerrit Viljoen, was conciliatory in tone and assisted in the search for a compromise. He stated that it was not the government's intention that the summit be a singular event, but that it should be seen as a first step in a series of meetings involving all concerned. He also indicated that the government would be prepared to attend a peace conference initiated or convened by religious leaders.[47] Chikane, Coleman, and the others who had been meeting continually during the previous two days[48] decided to convene a further meeting for the next morning, Sunday, May 19, and to invite additional participants. The meetings until then had been very informal, without mandate or status, and no minutes had been taken. They were more in the form of urgent get-togethers to exchange ideas and look for solutions.[49]

At the meeting on Sunday, more participants, such as Professor Johan Heyns, the former moderator of the Dutch Reformed Church, joined. The meeting identified the need to obtain feedback from political groupings about their attitude toward a joint initiative by church and business. Although in the public eye the church initiative to convene a further peace conference was continuing, the churches did not think that they were getting anywhere.[50] It was decided that a joint delegation of business and church leaders would seek a meeting with the state president and request that he postpone, or at least tone down, his peace summit to ensure that it would be perceived not as a single major event but as part of an ongoing process that would eventually bring the violence under control. The de Klerk peace summit was due in a week, and a meeting with him as well as the IFP and the ANC had to be held as soon as possible. A day later, the SACC met with Buthelezi and IFP representatives in Ulundi. This meeting was not successful. The IFP position remained that churches should not be facilitators in the peace process because of the SACC's close links with the ANC.[51]

On the following day, May 21, President de Klerk met the delegation of church and business leaders led by Chikane and Hall. De Klerk responded with irritation to the delegation's suggestions. He stressed that the government did not need the help of facilitators because it was in direct communication with all relevant parties. He did not regard the churches and business as having a mandate from the government to convene a peace conference; this remained the government's responsibility.[52] The meeting left no doubt that de Klerk's peace summit would proceed as planned.

Amid some apprehension about its outcome, the peace summit took place in Pretoria on May 24 and 25, 1991. Some 200 leading representatives from political groupings, churches, and the business community attended. The IFP and the Democratic Party were represented. Representatives from SACOB and CBM attended. Many government departments, self-governing states, and independent institutes were represented; the ANC, the PAC, the Azanian People's Organization (AZAPO), the Conservative Party, the SACC, and a few others were not. The explanation provided by most of those who did not attend, was that such a summit should be called by someone nonpartisan. It was clear that the peace summit would have an impediment from the outset because its decisions would not be binding on those not attending without their agreement.

On the first day of the summit, delegations delivered opening addresses to spell out their positions on political violence and to suggest possible solutions. Buthelezi, for example, called for peace and stressed that the peace process in South Africa would remain flawed unless relationships between the IFP and the ANC were normalized. He proposed a national campaign for peace and the establishment of a peace secretariat that should set up regional and local "peace action groups" throughout the country. These peace action groups should bring peace to troubled areas, counter rumor, provide channels of communication, and consult local leadership to facilitate peace moves.[53]

During discussions, Heyns proposed that the Rustenburg Conference church committee act as facilitator for an all-party conference to follow the peace summit.[54] The government, the IFP, and the ANC (although it was not present) indicated that they would consider this proposal. Delegates were unanimous about a code of conduct for political parties and security forces. "Peace talk hopes stay alive" is what newspapers reported after the first day.[55]

On the second day, analysts and experts briefed participants on the nature, extent, and causes of the violence. In an important move, the conference (and the state president) agreed to the appointment of Louw Alberts, cochairman of the Rustenburg Conference, to act as a one-man facilitating committee for a second peace conference with the power to include other members. He was asked because he was not an official church leader and because he was acceptable to de Klerk.[56] It was clearly understood that a more representative peace conference should follow and that Alberts would have to get together facilitators who were able to convene a more representative peace conference.

The peace summit took place without any major complications. The appointment of Alberts received wide support from most of the organizations that had not attended. The ANC welcomed these developments and said it regarded the peace process as being back on track. It stated that the process envisaged by the summit dovetailed closely with what the ANC had proposed.[57] "Stretch a point, call it success" was the view of the *Sunday Times*.[58] "It fell short of an exercise in national reconciliation. As a venture in peace-making, it was a start, not much more. If it has laid the basis for a second conference on violence, to which a greater range of participants may be attracted, it must be judged a success."

But while the peace process may have been back on track, political violence was on the increase. In May 1991, 336 persons died as a result of political violence.[59] It was the deadliest month to date.

Church and Business: Joint Facilitators

Alberts set about establishing a facilitating committee the very next day. He met with Chikane and others who had attended the earlier meetings between church and business leaders. Their task was to establish a committee in which all potential participants in a peace conference would have confidence. The idea was to create a balanced committee, with adequate representation from among black and white, male and female, left and right groups in South Africa. Chikane undertook to find names that would be acceptable to the ANC, the PAC, COSATU, AZAPO, the Communist Party, and other groups on the left, while Alberts sought representatives who would garner the trust of the government, business, and the IFP.[60] This was a major task because agreement on who should serve on the committee was necessary from at least the major political groupings before the committee was constituted. This agreement was reached in about a week. A facilitating committee of thirteen individuals[61] from church and business met and decided to work under a rotating chairperson. Most of the members knew each other and had established a degree of trust through earlier informal discussions. A new person on the facilitating committee was Sean Cleary, a business and political consultant who enjoyed the trust of the IFP. His presence on the committee helped secure full IFP participation.

During the process of establishing the facilitating committee, Alberts briefed de Klerk as progress was made. The president expressed his disappointment at the suggestion that several representatives from all parties were to be invited to the next peace conference. He believed that such a meeting would degenerate into a political debate and that it would be more fruitful to bring together Mandela, Buthelezi, and himself.[62] De Klerk felt that Alberts had compromised him but nevertheless gave him the go-ahead to proceed. Although Alberts did not argue this issue with the state president, it was his view that the leaders of political parties and groups should not do the negotiating. They would inevitably play the political positioning game to ensure that their constituencies would not perceive them as having given ground. At a time when de Klerk, Mandela, and Buthelezi had their minds fixed on the political arm wrestling that awaited them around the negotiating table, they were doing their best to project themselves as strong leaders with large support bases. None of them would have been keen to create the perception that they had made concessions to their opponents. Mandela feared that his more militant support base, consisting mainly of the youth and those supporters who were locked in conflict with the IFP in Natal, would regard a compromise with Buthelezi as a sign of retreat and therefore reject it. De Klerk wanted to prevent his supporters from drifting further toward the white right-wing parties and therefore could not afford to be seen as a person who was making too many concessions to "communists." As for Buthelezi, his beleaguered supporters in hostels and in many areas of Natal received their inspiration from Buthelezi's strong and uncompromising stand toward the ANC. This strongman image was an essential part of his style of leadership. Alberts was therefore of the view that second- and third-level leadership should do the negotiating, seeking consensus and reporting to their leaders. The leaders would make their input so that the negotiators could return to the

negotiations to seek new levels of consensus. Through continuous shut-
tling, consensus would ultimately be reached. During that process the
party leaders would give ground to achieve consensus but would not lose
face because they would not be perceived as being at the negotiations.[63]
This same approach was subsequently followed when the National
Peace Accord was negotiated.

The facilitating committee had the task of defining the next step.
Some groundwork had already been done. At the Sunday meeting of
May 19, Jay Naidoo from COSATU stressed that what was required was
a structured process that would bind parties to an agreement providing
a framework for ending the violence. This agreement needed to be the
culmination of a negotiating process because an event could not produce
the results. At the CBM offices, where the facilitating committee met,
Eloff and others were helping to conceptualize the process that would
have to be followed. Eloff's diagram (figure 1) reflects the thinking that
nonpartisan groups were well placed to contribute to the process. The
aim was to let the parties focus on the process rather than on the outcome (i.e., who the winner would be).[64] It was clear that at a peace conference, a code of conduct for political groups and for the security
forces would have to be discussed. The need for such codes of conduct
had been expressed before, including at de Klerk's peace summit.

The process that the facilitating committee decided to adopt followed
Eloff's diagram closely. A meeting, referred to by some as a "think tank
for peace" or "a preparatory meeting for a peace summit," to which all relevant political groups and some others were to be invited, was scheduled
for June 22, 1991. In line with its decision to operate on a very low-key
basis, the facilitating committee kept the plans about the forthcoming
meeting secret and made no announcements about its activities generally. CBM was charged with inviting delegations from political and trade
union groups across the spectrum. Leaks to the press about the planned
June 22 meeting caused some alarm, since leaks could cause some invi-
tees not to attend. The facilitating committee was forced to respond, but
merely confirmed that a meeting was being organized without spelling
out who had been invited or where the meeting would be held.[65] It was
soon established, however, that the meeting would be closed to the
media and that it would be held at the corporate headquarters of one of
South Africa's largest enterprises in Johannesburg.

The response from important political groups who were approached
for comment suggested that the planned meeting would be well

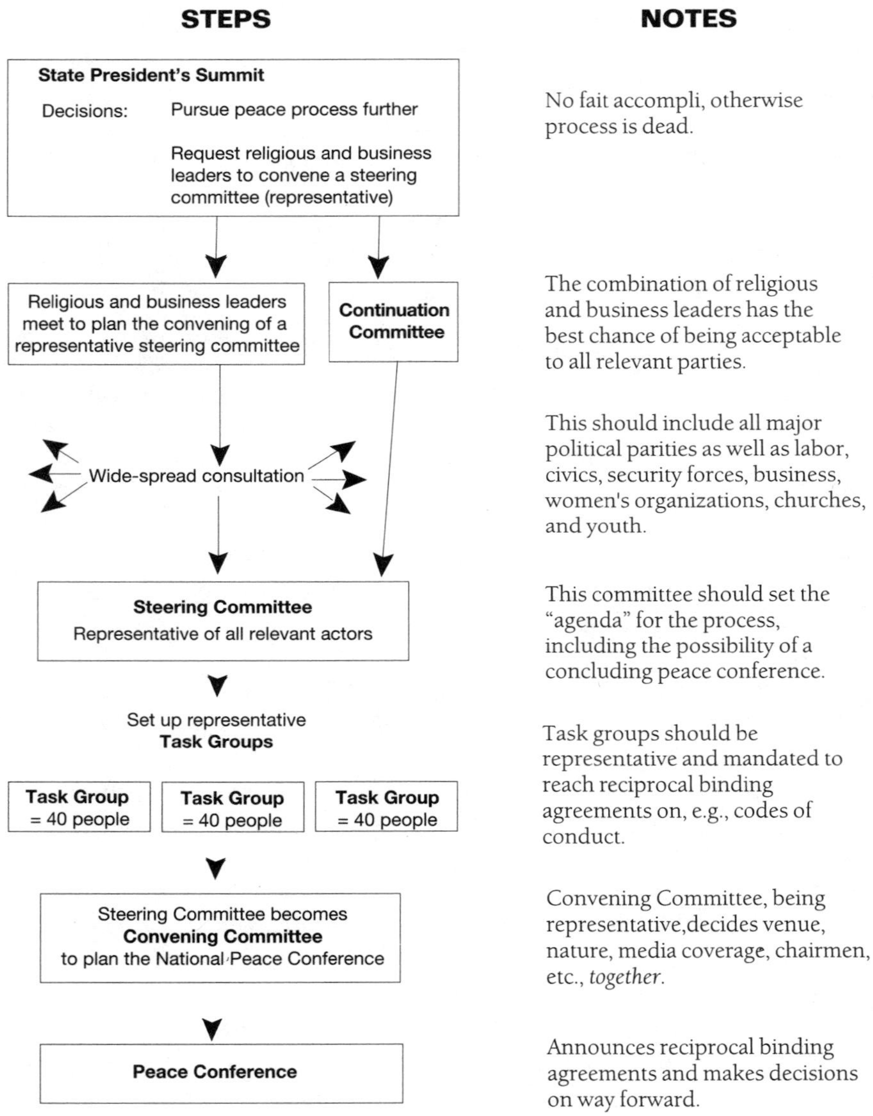

STEPS	NOTES

STEPS

State President's Summit

Decisions: Pursue peace process further

Request religious and business
leaders to convene a steering
committee (representative)

Religious and business leaders
meet to plan the convening of a
representative steering committee

**Continuation
Committee**

Wide-spread consultation

Steering Committee
Representative of all relevant actors

Set up representative
Task Groups

Task Group = 40 people	**Task Group** = 40 people	**Task Group** = 40 people

Steering Committee becomes
Convening Committee
to plan the National Peace Conference

Peace Conference

NOTES

No fait accompli, otherwise
process is dead.

The combination of religious
and business leaders has the
best chance of being acceptable
to all relevant parties.

This should include all major
political parities as well as labor,
civics, security forces, business,
women's organizations, churches,
and youth.

This committee should set the
"agenda" for the process,
including the possibility of a
concluding peace conference.

Task groups should be
representative and mandated to
reach reciprocal binding
agreements on, e.g., codes of
conduct.

Convening Committee, being
representative,decides venue,
nature, media coverage, chairmen,
etc., *together*.

Announces reciprocal binding
agreements and makes decisions
on way forward.

Figure 1. Possible peace process (prepared by Theuns Eloff)

attended. The country's two major trade union federations—COSATU and the National Congress of Trade Unions—as well as the Communist Party and the black-consciousness-aligned AZAPO, confirmed that they would attend. So did the Democratic Party. The South African government, the ANC, the PAC, and the IFP confirmed that they had been invited but declined to state whether they would attend. Very little was reported about the planned meeting—probably for fear of jeopardizing what was likely to be a sensitive meeting.

June 22 Peace Meeting: Start of a National Consensus

By the time June 22 arrived, it was clear that the attendance at the meeting would be beyond expectations. Only three white right-wing parties—the Conservative Party, the Herstigte Nasionale Party (Reestablished National Party), and the Afrikaner Weerstandsbeweging (Afrikaner Resistance Movement)—declined the invitation. For the first time ever the government, the ANC, and the IFP would sit at the same table to jointly talk about the violence. The leaders of the different parties were, however, not expected to attend. Until then, only two of the three organizations had met on any one occasion. It was also significant that the government and the PAC—the latter until then vigorously opposed to any negotiation involving the government—would meet officially for the first time. Expectations for the meeting were high even though not much was known about the planned proceedings. Headlines such as "Breakthrough in search for peace" appeared even before the meeting was held.[66] Leading participants felt that even if the only result from this planning meeting was the formation of a working group to continue to examine ways of dealing with violence, it would be a great step forward because it would keep the process alive. The great achievement, even before the meeting started, was seen to be the bringing together of such disparate players at the same table, even if the meeting did not come up with a solution for the violence.

Within the spacious facilities of the Barlow Rand headquarters in Sandton, Johannesburg, and without any presence of the media, an estimated 120 individuals representing about twenty organizations met on June 22, 1991, to talk about violence and peace. A detailed agenda for the meeting had not been made available to participants. Despite the outwardly relaxed appearance of the arriving participants, the gravity of the occasion was immediately brought home when the meeting was opened with a prayer by Archbishop Tutu, which referred to the country's destiny and to the future of millions of people who had placed their hopes in the hands of those attending. The prayer certainly set the tone for the meeting that was to follow. Archbishop Tutu also impressed upon the participants that if they were going to indulge in political discussions or squabbles, the meeting might as well stop and delegates go home. Violence, fear, and other issues to be discussed were far too serious to revert to political point scoring. The proposal that no participant be allowed to speak for more than five minutes was also accepted. The serious theme of the occasion, the participants' respect for the members of the facilitating committee, and the authority and standing of Archbishop Tutu were such that the politicians and all of us present accepted these "guidelines" without opposition. By rotating members of the facilitating committee as chairpersons, the organizers ensured that no one individual, interest, race, or political group could be perceived as dominating the proceedings or as directly or indirectly assisting another group. To ensure that no problems would result from the chairing of the meeting, two cochairs were presiding at all times.

The delegates then agreed to go through an exercise of identifying causes and key issues relating to political violence, as well as practical ways of ending it. By agreement, no debate was allowed, and all were encouraged to participate in the brainstorming exercise by stating their views and making suggestions in a summarized form. In rapid succession numerous opinions were offered about the causes of violence and ways to curtail it. The substance of what was said was noted on flip charts that were then attached to the walls of the meeting room. Participants quickly exhausted the possibilities. Every cause of political violence, as seen from the diverse political perspectives of those present, was listed on the flip charts. If a debate had been allowed about the merits or demerits of some of the points noted, the meeting would have exploded. In identifying the causes of violence, participants were forthright and often left no room for doubt about which party, individual, or authority they held responsible. Some fingers were inevitably pointed at individuals or organizations present, although not in a provocative or point-scoring manner. With great skill, Bobby Godsell, one of the cochairs at that stage, grouped the numerous points under headings to facilitate discussion about the way forward. The key recommendations that emerged included a code of conduct for political organizations, a code of conduct for security forces, and socioeconomic development and reconstruction, as well as enforcement mechanisms. The mechanisms suggested included a statutory standing commission and peace secretariats at national, regional, and community levels.[67]

The proposal was accepted that a preparatory committee be appointed to consider the information on the flip charts and to establish working groups that would draft proposals on those issues identified as necessary to end violence. Great progress had been made during the meeting thus far. Now came the tricky part—determining the members of the preparatory committee and how it would be constituted. Members of the facilitating committee (i.e., the church and business leaders) made it clear that in their view the new preparatory committee should consist of representatives from political parties present at the meeting. Proposals, counterproposals, accusations, and intense arguments arose. Some of the smallest parties were determined to have their representatives on the preparatory committee. When some parties argued for two representatives, others insisted that they should be entitled to three because of their bigger support base. The debate became more and more heated until, wisely, a cochair proposed an adjournment to let participants take a break and enjoy a finger supper and drinks. Something had to happen during the adjournment to defuse the situation and to bring forward a formula that was acceptable. The leaders of the delegations from three key political groups[68]—the ANC, the National Party, and the IFP—remained behind to discuss this matter among themselves.

When the meeting resumed, a joint proposal from the three groups was put to the meeting and accepted with audible relief. The preparatory committee would consist of the members of the existing facilitating committee and nine additional members, three each nominated by the ANC, the government, and the IFP. The new preparatory committee was to consult other relevant parties and organizations not represented at the meeting, with a view to convening an inclusive forum at which binding agreements would result. It would have to report progress to the various organizations represented by the first week of August. Having committed themselves to work for peace in South Africa, the organizations present agreed that no further matters ought to be discussed. There seemed to be a realization that the progress made could easily be undone by the raising of any new contentious topic. A spirit of cooperation had prevailed. The peace planning meeting had been a success.

The preparatory committee met two days later, on June 24, elected John Hall as chairperson, and decided to establish five working groups that would look at the following issues:

- Group 1: Code of conduct for political parties
- Group 2: Code of conduct for security forces
- Group 3: Socioeconomic development
- Group 4: Implementation and monitoring
- Group 5: Process, secretariat, and media

Each working group was to consist of three members from the government–National Party grouping, three members from the IFP, three members from the ANC-led alliance, one religious leader, and one business representative from the preparatory committee.[69] During the weeks that followed, each working group met on numerous occasions in an effort to produce a consensus document on the issue assigned to it.

The secretarial backup and coordination of this process was assigned to CBM, while the financial resources were provided by the government department responsible for constitutional development. Each working group produced draft documents that were then referred to the various principals for approval before being referred back to the negotiators to seek fresh consensus for a next draft. Taking into account the progress that was being made, the preparatory committee decided to fix Saturday, September 14, 1991, as the target date by which the reports from the five working groups had to be completed and on which a National Peace Convention would be held to ratify and sign the agreements. The National Peace Convention was planned as a high-profile leadership and media event to be held at a luxury hotel in central Johannesburg. South Africa's political, church, trade union, and business leaders were invited.

National Peace Convention: September 14, 1991

Under great pressure, and with only a few hours left before the National Peace Convention was to commence on September 14, the reports from the working groups were agreed to and collated to form what was from then on referred to as the National Peace Accord. Last-minute problems relating to the issues of cultural weapons, private armies (including Umkhonto we Sizwe, the military wing of the ANC), and a code of conduct for security forces could not be resolved and were therefore left vague or kept out of the NPA.

The National Peace Convention was a remarkable occasion. With the exception of three white right-wing parties,[70] the national leaders of all South Africa's political groups attended. This had never happened before. For the first time Mandela, de Klerk, and Buthelezi were together. Add to that the leaders of the South African Communist Party, the PAC, and numerous others, and it becomes clear why the National Peace Convention represented a breakthrough for South Africa. It showed that the deep-seated differences that existed would, in future, not prevent the various parties from speaking to each other about common interests. The occasion was so overwhelming that little thought was given to the three right-wing parties that were absent—something that could still haunt the peace process in future. They had been invited to attend but declined because they saw the meeting as a capitulation to the ANC and its allies. They regarded the ANC and the Communist Party as terrorist organizations that were responsible for the violence and therefore had to be dealt with through tough law-and-order methods.

Leaders of self-governing and independent states were there. So were leaders from various religious denominations, trade unions, and the business community, as well as the diplomatic corps, Zulu king Goodwill Zwelithini, traditional chiefs, and newspaper editors. The symbolic significance of such a gathering was powerful, something that the media conveyed with full fanfare.

With a large group of supporters of the Zulu king and the IFP gathered outside the hotel, armed with traditional weapons and chanting and singing, twenty-seven political, government, and trade union leaders inside the hotel solemnly signed the NPA, promising to uphold its provisions and to work for peace in South Africa. The leaders of the PAC and AZAPO, two Africanist-oriented groups on the left of the spectrum, declared their support for the spirit and objectives of the accord but declined to sign it because their strong noncollaborationist stance prevented them from being part of any structure in which the government was represented. They did, however, declare themselves in favor of peace and undertook to promote it.

With the signing of the NPA, an important stage had been reached in the process that aimed at creating peace. South Africa's leaders, with the exception of elements on the extreme right and left, signed a contract to jointly pursue this objective. Maybe the agreement ought to have been called "Accord to Achieve Peace" rather than the "National Peace Accord." Peace had not arrived in the country, and the high expectations that arose from the events at the National Peace Convention would certainly not be met if the public believed that the signing of a document would suddenly do away with political violence in South Africa. The document was, however, "one of the few consensual documents to have emerged in South Africa"[71] and therefore had the potential of effectively addressing the violence. It remained to be seen whether the necessary commitment, resources, and hard work would be forthcoming to actually realize the objectives of the NPA.

3

ASSESSMENT
OF THE
PROCESS

Role of Professionals and Practitioners

The process described thus far may well contain some useful material for experts and professionals to analyze and comment on. I shall not attempt a detailed analysis but will highlight some aspects of the process and, with the benefit of hindsight, assess them from a practitioner's point of view.

By "practitioners" I mean those who through circumstances, and without any specialized training, have found themselves in positions where they have actively participated in attempts to manage or resolve a conflict. By "professionals" I mean experts who have made conflict and its resolution their special field of study, equipping themselves with an expertise that the public is entitled to expect from a professional. Obviously there are many examples of professionals becoming involved in attempts to manage or resolve actual conflicts. These persons should perhaps be described as professional practitioners, but I shall not attempt to devise strict definitions and will stick to the two general categories of practitioners and professionals.

My personal experience is limited to involvement in social and political conflicts in South Africa. Practitioners and professionals in that country have had only limited contact and interaction with each other. The scarcity of professionals in South Africa to address community and political conflicts, and their failure to use their expertise to the fullest by applying it to actual conflict, limits the chances that practitioners will deal with conflicts in a creative, effective, and timely manner. As a result, the cost at which satisfactory results are eventually achieved is probably unnecessarily high, and the positive results do not last as long as they otherwise would. The invaluable role that someone with skills in conflict resolution can play is illustrated by the impact of the diagram produced for CBM by Theuns Eloff. The attempt to conceptualize the complicated peace process that lay ahead proved to be absolutely crucial for the success of that part of the process covered by the diagram. Eloff, although not a professional in the field of conflict resolution, was experienced enough to encapsulate the essence of a most complicated planned process in a one-page diagram. His diagram and the thinking behind it had a significant influence on the facilitating committee, as is clear from the close resemblance between the proposals set out in Eloff's diagram and the actual process that followed. The committee developed and implemented the proposed process to the stage at which the NPA was signed.

Individuals who understand the political dynamics operating in conflict situations, who know the personalities of key players, who understand the sensitivities and the importance of process, who are trusted, and who are not formally aligned with any of the political groups involved can therefore play a crucial role in assisting the parties and other practitioners in constructively dealing with conflicts. These skills, which develop primarily through involvement and experience, and not only through the study of conflict resolution techniques, are present within many of the nongovernmental organizations in South Africa. They ought to be tapped to a far greater extent and, where possible, be augmented by the acquisition of conflict resolution skills from available experts and literature. Many of those who have equipped themselves with such skills have in the past been involved mainly in industrial and labor disputes. They have acted as facilitators during wage negotiations and as mediators during strikes. Only recently has some of the emphasis shifted to community conflict.

If we examine the actors involved in the attempts to bring together the relevant political parties around the issue of violence in South Africa—namely, political, church, and business leaders, as well as government—not one of the individuals involved can be described as a professional. There were, however, some who had developed a very finely tuned feeling for the complexities and sensitivities involved in such a process. None of them, to my knowledge, had any formal training or specialization in conflict management or peace building. Their actions were determined by intuition rather than by a plan of action derived from existing conflict resolution models. Both church and business leaders had been exposed to conflicts and involved in dealing with them on numerous occasions. Church leaders had played crucial roles in managing conflict and mediating between security forces and township dwellers during the years of serious political revolt in the 1980s. The experience of business leaders originated not so much from involvement in the township violence or community clashes with the police (they had remained fairly aloof from that), but from having to negotiate with strong and often militant trade unions. Dealing with strikes and industrial action by unions became part of a business leader's job during the 1980s. These experiences helped greatly in equipping church and business leaders with the skills necessary to act as facilitators and mediators, but they were not sufficient to avoid all mistakes.

Role of Government

When President de Klerk announced his planned peace summit on April 18, he stressed that it would be inclusive, but he failed to seek support for the idea even among the more important players. The government, as a major party in the political violence and with allegations that it was partly responsible for fueling it, should have known that such a unilateral announcement would be met with grave suspicion by its principal political opponents. Questions about de Klerk's political agenda immediately arose. He was known to be a shrewd tactician, and political opponents are wary of moves that are not transparent. A successful summit by de Klerk would have placed him on the moral high ground on the issue of violence when, in the eyes of many, he was partly responsible for it. De Klerk had not followed the right process and should have known that without prior consultation with key actors his move would be viewed as a political trick.

For one of the parties in a conflict to also act as facilitator in bringing the various conflicting groups together is unusual and unlikely to work. De Klerk's motives may have been perfectly noble, but the good old days, when the government could make unilateral decisions, were over, and he had failed to appreciate the new dynamics of the transition. Consultation and joint decision making were now the order of the day. In many of the political steps he had taken he appeared to be perfectly aware of this, but occasionally he reverted to procedures that enabled him to keep a firm grip on the process. Why else would President de

Klerk have been disappointed with Alberts for establishing a large facilitating committee instead of a committee consisting of the ANC, the IFP, and the government, as he had hoped for? De Klerk appeared reluctant to lose control over the process and did not fully appreciate that only if that happened would the prospects for success be good. It was only when it became apparent that his peace summit would fail without the presence of the ANC and other key groups that he agreed to scale down the profile and expected outcome of the summit and allow it to become the start of a process, which it did.

De Klerk carried the ultimate responsibility for the maintenance of law and order in the country but was no longer in a position to do so without the cooperation of other political groups. Neither he nor any of the other key political leaders was therefore capable of bringing opposing political groups together to find answers to the violence. They were each part of the problem. Those with clean hands as far as violence was concerned—namely, civil society leaders from church and business—were the only ones acceptable to all groups as mediators and facilitators. De Klerk's security forces and the supporters of Mandela and Buthelezi were directly implicated in much of the violence. They had therefore lost the trust and confidence of their political opponents and forfeited any chance of being accepted as mediators.

Role of the Church

Organs of civil society are often well placed to act as mediators or facilitators in conflict situations. In South Africa, with its highly fragmented, polarized, and politicized landscape, there are very few institutions, even in civil society, that can be considered independent or nonaligned. Therefore, to find institutions of civil society able to act as independent mediators or facilitators is not easy. Suspicions abound as far as the role of the church is concerned. When, in March 1991, the SACC called for an urgent national meeting "of all leaders of strife-torn communities within a week," it should have known that they were embarking on a venture that would be looked upon with great suspicion by some of the players. The South African government, for example, suspected that by referring to "all leaders of strife-torn communities" the SACC was conveying that the government would not be welcome at the proposed national meeting because only black political leaders who had support in townships affected by the violence were invited. If the proposed meeting was to be a serious attempt to deal with the violence, then the political groups and organizations directly involved in or affected by the violence should be part of it. Clearly the government, which controlled the security forces, the courts, and the purse strings, was a key player and would have to be present. The SACC had given the impression that it wanted to be exclusive rather than inclusive by keeping the government out and thus had raised government doubts about the SACC's impartiality as a mediator.

What the SACC further omitted to do before its announcement of the planned meeting was to canvass some of the key actors involved. It is clear that Chief Minister Buthelezi and the IFP, for example, had not been briefed. The history of tensions and antagonism between Buthelezi and the SACC should have been a warning that Buthelezi was likely to reject participation in such a meeting unless he could be persuaded to become part of it through prior discussions. Again, to talk about violence and peace without IFP representation would have made no sense. Buthelezi's response was almost predictable. He attacked "naive" churchmen and accused them of trying to take charge of the peace process. The attempt by the SACC to call the first national meeting on violence was therefore stillborn. The church leaders had not given enough attention to the process and had excluded important players. What should also have been clear is that as long as the SACC and Buthelezi remained at arm's length, the SACC, and therefore the church, would not be acceptable as the sole facilitator or mediator in bringing the main players together.

The SACC repeated the same mistake six weeks later when, on May 9, Chikane announced that church leaders were planning a national peace conference for "affected communities" excluding the government. He announced that church leaders would be speaking to Buthelezi to persuade him to take part in the conference. For the same reasons as before, the IFP response was predictable, and the initiative never became reality.

Role of Business

During 1990 and 1991, CBM was preparing itself for a role as a national facilitator and mediator. It followed the correct route of quietly equipping itself with all the information relating to the violence and then arranging low-key meetings with the ANC, the government, the IFP, and others. The process was correct, but the question was whether the business sector as a whole would have enough credibility to be accepted as a trustworthy facilitator and mediator. After all, CBM represented only a small, albeit influential, part of the greater business community. It constituted the more progressive elements and was doing its best to influence the greater business sector to move in its direction. The negative response that South Africa's business leaders gave to the address by Mandela at their meeting on May 16 and SACOB's open canvassing for de Klerk's peace summit were reasons for the ANC to distrust the business sector. Businessmen regarded Mandela as unpragmatic and unreasonable.[72] This important sector of civil society, although not formally aligned with any political party, was still too closely associated with vested interests and the status quo to be acceptable to all parties as a mediator or facilitator. For both the church and the business sectors it was clear that on their own they would not be able to take the peace process any further.

Role of the Church and Business Combined

The key to breaking the logjam and pulling disparate political groups together proved to be the joining of forces by churches and organized business. The fact that this happened only when it became obvious to both that on their own they would fail suggests that the cooperation was determined by necessity and not by choice or noble considerations. Church and business had each hoped to bring the political parties together on their own initiatives and thus to take the credit for any progress. Egos play a role even among peacemakers, facilitators, and mediators.

A feeling of helplessness and desperation seemed to have led Chikane and Coleman to propose joint action when they met on May 17. The responsibility of civil society structures was part of their discussion. So was the point that both church and business had a direct interest in seeing South Africa move successfully through its transition toward a new democracy. Their decision to discuss this matter with other business, church, and trade union representatives led to the establishment of the facilitating committee, which produced a breakthrough. Civil society found a formula for maximizing its influence and role and for positioning itself where it ought to be positioned—namely, outside the sphere of formal party politics, where it could hold politicians accountable and influence their decisions because of the strong grassroots support and influence that civil society organs have. The addition of trade unions to the combination of church and business would have added further weight had the largest trade union federation, COSATU, not been in close and formal alliance with the ANC. It would have upset the delicate balance that church and business had achieved if labor unions had become part of the facilitating committee. Unions did, however, play an important behind-the-scenes role and were frequently part of discussions with church and business.[73]

It was known to everyone that individuals within these elements of civil society, and those who eventually served on the facilitating committee, had leanings toward different political groups. The composition of the facilitating committee was designed in a way that persuaded most relevant political groups that there were committee members who would be sympathetic to their causes. The balance was such that each political group in the country felt satisfied that its interests would be protected on the facilitating committee. Not that the political groups expected committee members to espouse party or political positions, but the knowledge that there would be a brake on actions that would disadvantage a particular party was sufficient reason to entrust the committee with its task. Neither the church nor business were formally aligned with any political group, and it was known that within each of these institutions various political views were held. Ensuring that these views were represented around the table demonstrated the good faith of the committee as a whole. Leaders and key figures with credibility from within the church and organized business, two important elements of civil society, were therefore largely responsible for the success of the first inclusive meeting of South African leaders on the issue of political violence.

4

THE
NATIONAL
PEACE
ACCORD

Content

In a comprehensive document, divided into ten short chapters, the NPA set out a vision for a new democracy, peace, and stability and provided for the establishment of a nationwide network of peace committees and other structures to realize these objectives (see appendix for the complete text). The accord acknowledged that the common goal of a multi-party democracy would be impossible to attain in a climate of violence, intimidation, and fear and that certain fundamental rights needed to be recognized and upheld to ensure democratic political activity. Universally accepted fundamental rights such as freedom of conscience, speech, association, and assembly and free participation in peaceful political activity were spelled out and endorsed.

The signatories recognized that political violence was threatening democratization in South Africa. They committed themselves to end the political violence and to make the country one in which all could live, work, and play together in peace and harmony. Key provisions in the accord are described below:

Code of Conduct for Political Parties and Organizations
Political intolerance was regarded by many as one of the prime underlying causes of the violence. South Africa had never experienced free political activity for all and had not developed a culture of democracy. A code of conduct for political parties was therefore not a mere nicety, but

was regarded as absolutely essential for setting norms and standards where none existed. The code promoted political tolerance and called on all parties to publicly condemn political violence (see chapter 2 of the accord). Detailed instructions were provided to regulate the relations between political groups and those between political groups and various authorities such as the police or local authorities.

Code of Conduct for Security Forces

The security forces, particularly the South African Police, had over many years become a controversial factor in the violence that plagued the country. A record of suspicion and distrust, primarily from black South Africans, had built up and severely damaged relations between black communities and the police. This distrust undermined the ability of the police to maintain law and order and to deal effectively with political violence. The police were seen by many as the implementors of apartheid and therefore biased.

Despite this history, the signatories to the National Peace Accord envisaged a key role for the police in peacekeeping efforts and in maintaining law and order. The code of conduct for the police was aimed at promoting sound policing practices and establishing a cooperative relationship between the police and communities (see chapters 3 and 4 of the accord). Concepts such as the minimum use of force and the equal treatment of all citizens were elaborated on in the code of conduct. Political neutrality was stressed and guidelines were provided for police involvement in the structures to be set up under the accord. A similar code of conduct for the South African Defence Forces was attempted but could not be finalized and therefore does not form part of the accord.[74]

National Peace Committee (NPC)

Composed of top representatives from all signatories to the accord, the NPC, in practice, consists of approximately sixty individuals. It has the task of monitoring the implementation of the NPA, resolving disputes over contraventions of the code of conduct for political parties, and assuming responsibility for socioeconomic reconstruction and development (see chapter 8 of the accord). Decisions are made by consensus, a requirement that makes it difficult to deal with contentious issues. These issues frequently revolve around political differences and are only resolved through lengthy discussions and compromises. Making decisions by consensus encourages smaller parties to remain part of the committee; under a voting procedure, some of those voted down would storm out and not return.

National Peace Secretariat (NPS)

The NPS is responsible for establishing, coordinating, servicing, and financing the countrywide network of regional dispute resolution committees (RDRCs) and local dispute resolution committees (LDRCs) (see chapter 7 of the accord). Eight of its nine members are nominated by the NPC to ensure that a spectrum of political interests is represented. The ninth member is an official from the Department of Justice. Under the NPA, the NPS was to become a statutory body served by a full-time secretariat and funded by the Department of Justice.[75] Members of the NPS were then formally appointed by the state president to serve in that capacity for a term of three years on a part-time basis.

Regional and Local Dispute Resolution Committees

What the accord envisaged was that the country would be divided into regions and that within each region an RDRC would be established by the NPS (see chapter 8 of the accord). These committees were made up of regional representatives from political organizations, the church, trade unions, commerce, and industry, as well as representatives from local and tribal authorities, the police, and the defense forces. Their legitimacy was derived from their representativeness. The task of the RDRCs is to assist in preventing violence and intimidation at the regional level and to establish LDRCs within their regions. The accord aims to establish LDRCs in as many villages, townships, and towns as possible. The composition of the LDRCs reflects the needs and concerns of the community at the grassroots level. They have an important peacemaking and peace-building role. They deal with the settling of disputes that cause public violence or intimidation, they pursue local peace accords, and they serve as liaisons with local authorities regarding the holding of rallies, marches, and other gatherings.

Commission of Inquiry Regarding the Prevention of Public Violence and Intimidation

Commonly referred to as the Goldstone Commission after its chairman Justice Richard Goldstone, this commission was established by an act of Parliament a few months before the NPA was signed. The reference to this commission in the accord is significant because the signatories thereby endorsed the nature, terms of reference, and composition of the commission (see chapter 6 of the accord). Wide consultation with political and other interest groups took place before the members of the Goldstone Commission were appointed. Its function is to inquire into incidents of political violence, its nature, and its causes and to establish who is responsible. The commission is also expected to recommend steps that would prevent public violence and intimidation. It is equipped with legal powers such as the power to subpoena witnesses and to enter premises.

Socioeconomic Reconstruction and Development

To contribute to peace building, the socioeconomic reconstruction and development envisaged by the accord was very much grassroots oriented and focused on communities detrimentally affected by political violence (see chapter 5 of the accord). It was also aimed at potential flash point areas, such as squatter settlements, to defuse tensions and prevent violence. In many areas afflicted by political violence, homes have been damaged or destroyed, and fleeing residents have become refugees. The premise of the NPA is that assistance with the reconstruction of homes and basic facilities in such cases would contribute to peace. Communities become involved in development tasks through subcommittees that link up with RDRCs or LDRCs in the area. The accord envisaged that socioeconomic development with community involvement would lead to a measure of stability. Normal developmental work would remain the government's responsibility.

Police Board

The main objective of the Police Board is to promote more effective policing and better relations between the police and communities (see chapter 3.3 of the accord). It is composed of members of the public and police officers in equal numbers. It has no executive powers and makes recommendations to the minister of law and order on policy issues. The members of the public are nominated by the NPC to ensure broad political representation.

The accord further provides for the appointment of justices of the peace, for special criminal courts, and for mechanisms to deal with breaches of the NPA. At the grassroots level, breaches of the provisions of the accord are to be dealt with by the parties themselves through "mediation, arbitration and adjudication." The NPC is charged with handling alleged breaches of the code of conduct for political parties. Matters that the NPC cannot resolve must be referred to an arbitrator who "shall be a person with legal skills, appointed by the relevant parties by consensus, failing which the arbitrator shall be appointed by the National Peace Committee." The arbitrator may order an organization to remedy the breach. The fact that the NPA is an agreement entered into by the signatories and not a document that can be enforced by statute has rendered the enforcement provisions of the accord ineffective as a sanction, something that has continuously hampered the NPC in acting against transgressors of the code of conduct.

Implementation: Peace Structures

Political parties presumably exist for the purpose of pursuing political power that enables them to implement their policy programs. The same applies to the political groups that signed the NPA. During the period leading to the signing of the NPA, the political groups and other participants showed a keen interest and were intensely involved in the process. Once the accord was signed, however, that interest and involvement from political leaders was largely diverted to the new item on the national agenda, the coming multiparty negotiations for a new constitution. The National Peace Convention on September 14 had been a historic occasion, but many political leaders regarded it as a major event—the concluding act of a process—rather than the start of the implementation process for the NPA. The anticipated constitutional negotiations were the next main objective, leaving the implementation of the NPA as a secondary matter further down on the agenda. While the signing of the NPA had led to a major breakthrough for South Africa—the creation of sufficient confidence and trust among the parties to clear the way for constitutional negotiations—the signatories' enthusiasm for proceeding with this task caused them to fall into the trap of neglecting the postagreement stage of the accord. As Colin Coleman of CBM aptly put it, "I think that after the NPA was signed, the focus of the people was 'OK, we've got the Peace Accord, now let's move on to negotiations' rather than 'OK, we've got the accord, let's work out how to implement it.'"[76]

Within three months, on December 20, 1991, multiparty negotiations commenced with the first meeting of the Convention for a Democratic South Africa (CODESA), a forum of nineteen parties. The peace process had played an important role in getting the political groups that far.

The implementation of the provisions of the NPA required the full cooperation of all the signatories at local, regional, and national levels. Never before had any such joint venture been attempted. During decades of minority rule, the country had become used to the unilateral imposition of new policies or projects by the government. It was a novel experience for both those with and those without political power to now work for the NPA as equals on the basis of mutual respect. Decisions on the implementation of the accord had to be made by consensus. Skin color or the fact someone happened to be a member of the government was no longer a criterion. This approach was followed when the implementation stage of the NPA began. Logistically it was a daunting task. The aim was to create a nationwide network of peace structures in a society that was deeply divided and in which political violence was continuing unabated. Even a year before the signing of the accord, no one would have given such an undertaking any chance of success. The cooperation of the signatories cleared the way for implementation at the regional and local levels, but a start was made at the national level with the NPC.

National Peace Committee

After the September 1991 signing of the NPA, party representatives from the signatories were given the task of assisting with the implementation of the NPA.

The NPC was created by each of the signatories providing one or, in the case of the larger parties, two members to serve on the committee. This was not a difficult task, as many of the individuals concerned had been involved in shaping the NPA and so knew each other and were familiar with the objective of the exercise. A large NPC consisting of approximately sixty individuals was the result. Most members of the committee were senior and experienced politicians.[77] John Hall, outgoing president of SACOB, was elected chairperson. He had been a member of the earlier facilitating committee and was respected by the signatories for his impartiality in steering difficult meetings through crises with a combination of tact, a sense of humor, and expertise. The vice-chairperson was Bishop Stanley Magoba, president of the Methodist Church of South Africa and a former political prisoner who had been imprisoned on Robben Island. Magoba was known to have had leanings toward the

PAC in the past, but this never surfaced as a relevant factor during his election as vice-chairperson. He was highly regarded for his ceaseless efforts to promote peace and reconciliation among all South Africans.

National Peace Secretariat

The most pressing task for the NPC was the nomination of members of the NPS, which was the committee responsible for establishing the RDRCs and LDRCs. There was an urgency to get these regional and local structures off the ground, as violence was continuing to take its toll. The high media profile accorded to the signing of the NPA on September 14, 1991, had raised expectations that the accord would be able to make a decisive impact within a relatively short time. But the selection of members for the NPS proved to be more time-consuming and arduous than anticipated. It took more than six weeks from the signing of the accord before unanimity was reached on the composition of the NPS. Suspicion that one group would have more influence on the NPS than another caused the ANC, IFP, and government representatives to indulge in constant horse trading about whom to include. The political weight of these three parties allowed them to dominate decision making within the NPA structures. Once they reached agreement on an issue, it was highly unlikely that anyone else would manage to change that decision. Other signatories would fall into line.

The NPS was eventually constituted on November 8, 1991. It included one representative each from the ANC alliance, the National Party, the IFP, the Democratic Party, the Labour Party, and the legal profession— each one endorsed by the signatories to the accord—and one member from the Department of Justice.[78] Attempts were made to add a representative from the right-wing Conservative Party, but the party made it clear that it had no intention of serving on NPA structures. Although the Conservatives had refused to attend the National Peace Convention and sign the accord, their participation in NPA structures was regarded as important. For this reason the representatives of the ANC alliance, the National Party, and the IFP who negotiated the composition of the NPS decided to keep the remaining four positions vacant, with the hope that at some future date it would become possible to persuade both the Conservative Party, on the right, and the PAC, on the left, to become part of the NPS.

The seven members of the NPS had to choose a chair from within their ranks and elected Antonie Gildenhuys. He had a distinguished career in the legal profession, had previously been the president of the Transvaal Law Society, and was a partner in one of the top legal firms in Johannesburg.

The task of implementing the NPA could then start in all earnestness. An office was opened in Pretoria with support staff supplied by the Department of Justice. Funds were made available by the same department, although the NPS was not told how much had been set aside. Requests for funds or other resources had to be submitted to the department, which would then decide on the matter. The Department's approach was that all reasonable requests in line with the objectives of the NPA would be granted. Departmental officials by and large abided by this rule, although the normal bureaucratic red tape of a government agency often caused delays and frustrations.

The NPS, in consultation with the signatories, identified eleven regions that together covered the entire country but excluded four of the apartheid-created independent states—the Transkei, Bophuthatswana, Ciskei, and Venda (figure 2).[79] These states had not signed the NPA and therefore had not agreed to the establishment of structures within their territories. The immediate task was to establish RDRCs, particularly in the violence-torn Natal-KwaZulu Region and the area around Johannesburg normally referred to as the Witwatersrand-Vaal Region.[80] This proved to be a difficult task, particularly in those areas where violence was rife and where, consequently, deep antagonism existed between supporters of different political groups or communities and the security forces.

Regional Dispute Resolution Committees

The regional leaders of the organizations referred to in chapter 7 of the NPA were invited to attend exploratory meetings to discuss the establishment of RDRCs. Each region required a different approach because of political, demographic, historical, and other differences. The fact that senior members of, for example, the IFP and the ANC alliance were represented on the NPS meant that in those areas where the two organizations were key players the two members of the NPS could prepare the way by explaining to their respective regional leadership what the meetings were all about and generally attempting to secure their cooperation. The fact that their party leaders had signed the NPA did not necessarily mean that leadership at the regional or local level would

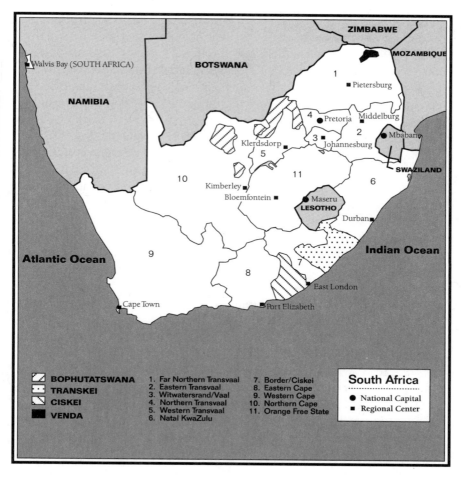

Figure 2. The eleven NPA regions (under the new constitution, the four "independent" states listed at bottom left have been reincorporated into South Africa)

gloss over existing enmities or that they would slavishly follow party
lines. They had to be persuaded, and it sometimes required intervention
from the senior party leadership to do so.

The preparatory meetings that were organized and attended by the
NPS in the different regions were often tense, crisis ridden, and confron-
tational. Recriminations against the police or against another political

group present often led to explosions and adjournments. The meetings were normally chaired by the NPS chairperson or other members of the NPS. Parties sometimes walked out or refused to attend unless a particular issue was addressed. Long disputes could develop about the composition of the RDRC, with the issue being whether a particular organization had sufficient support and standing to be regarded as relevant in the region. In many cases it was necessary to hold a number of exploratory meetings before an RDRC could be constituted. All the facilitation and mediation skills the NPS could muster were required to save some meetings from complete disintegration.

It must be borne in mind that in many instances representatives from organizations that had refused to meet in the past or between whom a deep hatred existed were suddenly being asked to sit around the same table and to serve on the same committee as though nothing had happened in the past and as though historical animosities could all just be set aside. For example, an ANC representative at such an exploratory meeting might recognize the police representative as the person who had personally tortured him while he was imprisoned without trial. Should that be forgotten and ignored, or should the matter be raised and dealt with? These were difficult issues that had to be overcome. Decisions had to be made by consensus. That made it difficult, for example, to decide who the chairperson or the cochairpersons should be and what the executive should look like.

By the middle of December 1991, however, RDRCs had been established in the Witwatersrand-Vaal, Natal-KwaZulu, and Western Cape Regions. The composition of these committees differed from region to region, and membership ranged from twenty-five to sixty. Because most members of the committees had strong political affiliations, the role of chairperson inevitably fell on the shoulders of those who were not openly tied to any political party—churchmen, businessmen, and to a lesser extent academics. In Natal, for example, after lengthy deliberations, the committee decided to appoint two cochairpersons, both whites. They were a prominent businessman, M. C. Pretorius (who happened to be a member of the National Consultative Group of CBM) and Archbishop Denis Hurley, a prominent antiapartheid campaigner from the Catholic Church.

Once an RDRC had been established, an office and staff had to be found and the important task of establishing LDRCs in the region had to be addressed.

Local Dispute Resolution Committees

The process of establishing LDRCs repeated itself in the various regions on numerous occasions during 1992 and is still in progress. Hundreds of meetings were held throughout the country, and many successes and mistakes occurred. By the end of September 1993, more than two years after the signing of the NPA, 11 regional peace committees (RPCs) and 180 local peace committees (LPCs) had been established.[81] A further 30 LPCs were in the process of being established. Numerous regional and local offices were operating, and the paid staff complement of the peace structures throughout the country stood at 239 in November 1993. Some 8,500 volunteers, consisting of members of the various peace committees, monitors, and other helpers, were attached to the NPA structures to try to make them work. Extensive efforts were under way to provide training for these volunteers. They needed to be equipped with the skills to carry out their mission effectively. The training focused on imparting skills in facilitation, mediation, and conflict management.

Infrastructure and Resources

The amount the government budgeted for the 1993/94 financial year for the activities of the NPS, the RPCs, and the LPCs was R41.175 million ($12.2 million) (see table 1).[82]

In addition to this amount, funds were made available by the Danish and British governments for training and communication equipment, respectively. For the first eighteen months after the signing of the accord, all funds required for the peace structures were paid directly from the Department of Justice or the Department of Finance. This led to a perception that the peace structures were under the control of the government, with the implication that manipulation could take place or was taking place. In addition, the risk of hampering efforts by peace committees with red tape became very real, particularly with funds of such magnitude involved. Complaints in this regard came from various structures. In an effort to shorten unnecessarily cumbersome procedures required by government financial regulations for the handling of public funds, and to become more visibly independent from the government, agreement was reached that starting June 1993 the NPS would administer the funds budgeted for its activities through its own account in accordance with agreed procedures. The Goldstone Commission

Table 1. National Peace Secretariat budget, 1993/ 94 (millions)

Salaries *(secretariat office, regional and local offices)*	R11.118	($3.3)
Administrative expenses *(subsistence allowances, travel, telephone bills, training, seminar expenses, advertisements, government levies)*	R10.913	($3.2)
Stock *(pamphlets, posters, stationery, and uniforms)*	R2.896	($0.9)
Equipment *(office machines, recording and transcription machines, radios, furniture, computers and terminals, vehicles, photocopiers, distinctive clothing and symbols)*	R6.114	($1.8)
Professional services *(maintenance, programming, remuneration for members of committees, accommodations, facilitators)*	R10.134	($3.0)
Total	R41.175	($12.2)

operated independently of the NPC and the NPS and therefore had its own budgetary and staff arrangements.

A sophisticated marketing and peace promotion campaign was developed by a marketing subcommittee with the involvement of some of South Africa's top advertising agencies. A peace logo and radio, press, and television promotions were launched nationwide through this committee.

In many areas of the country, facilitators had to be appointed on a paid basis to assist in the establishment of committees or to facilitate and mediate in a conflict or dispute that had arisen. These were usually individuals who had received some training in conflict management and who had gained experience in industrial relations through an involvement in industrial disputes, strikes, and negotiations. Few people in South Africa were formally trained in dealing with community conflicts and disputes.

A major part of the work of the NPS and the peace committees revolved around facilitating disputes and managing conflicts. These disputes or conflicts could arise for a variety of reasons, including the withholding of permission for political marches and rallies, police conduct during marches and rallies, attempts by one political group to prevent another from engaging in political activities, disputes between taxi associations over taxi routes, threatened or actual consumer boycotts or refusal to pay for municipal services such as water and electricity, and threats to withdraw the provision of these services. Hundreds of conflicts over these and other issues were addressed by the peace committees throughout the country.

In the small, conservative town of Warmbad, in the Northern Transvaal Region, for example, the LPC, together with a facilitator brought in from the NPS, defused a conflict during April 1993 that could have resulted in bloodshed. Tensions in the adjoining black township of Bela-Bela ran high as a result of dissatisfaction with poor basic services and the rates that the white local authority of Warmbad had imposed for such services. A protest march by residents of Bela-Bela, organized by civic organizations and the local branch of the ANC, was planned to proceed from the township across the railway line to the municipal buildings in the white town of Warmbad. Permission for the march had been refused by the local authority of Warmbad, and armed right-wing vigilante groups belonging to the Afrikaaner Weerstandsbeweging threatened to use violence to prevent any march from crossing the railway line. On a Friday morning thousands of black residents marched toward Warmbad. Since a violent clash between the protesters and the armed right-wingers was expected, about fifty policemen from the internal stability unit were stationed at the railway line between the oncoming crowd and scores of supporters of the Afrikaaner Weerstandsbeweging. The right-wingers were threatening to call for reinforcements from the farmers and other supporters who had gathered in the town. Frantic members of the LPC managed to persuade the leaders of the march to pause shortly before they reached the railway line to attempt last-minute negotiations with the police and officials from the local administration. For ten hours thereafter the facilitator and members of the LPC criss-crossed the railway line in an attempt to facilitate an agreement that could defuse the impending clash. On a number of occasions the impatient crowd threatened to proceed with the march, while the right-wingers waited, ready for action. Finally, at 6:00 p.m., an agreement was reached to postpone the payment of service rates. Armed with this agreement, members of the LPC managed to persuade the crowd, still in the thousands, to turn back to Bela-Bela. A crisis had been defused, no violence had taken place, and nothing was reported in the media. As far as the South African public was concerned, it had been a non-event.

A further example of the role played by LPC occurred in the mining town of Phalaborwa in the Eastern Transvaal Region. At the beginning of 1993 the mining company had allocated some houses in the white part of Phalaborwa to some of its black employees. This move immediately caused conflict in the community. White residents threatened to prevent blacks from moving in, while the black community from the adjoining township organized a consumer boycott of all white businesses. The local authority reported this worsening conflict to the RPC, which immediately set about establishing an LPC made up of representatives from all local interest groups (including the Conservative Party). Within a very short period a training workshop for the new LPC was held to equip the members with conflict resolution skills. Two weeks later the LPC had managed to negotiate the Greater Phalaborwa Peace Accord, a comprehensive document that addressed not only the mining company's decision to allocate houses to its black employees and the consumer boycott, but also a range of other issues that did, or could, cause tensions in the community. The document was signed by all relevant groups in the town, including churches and organized business. Blacks could move into the allocated houses without hindrance, the consumer boycott was called off, normality returned to the town, and a new structure existed through which all potential conflicts could be addressed jointly.

Two years after the signing of the NPA, good progress had been made on the implementation of many of its provisions. Aspects provided for in the accord but not yet implemented included a code of conduct for the South African Defence Forces, the establishment of self-protection units in communities, the appointment of justices of the peace, the establishment of special criminal courts, and the implementation of the provisions on the carrying of dangerous weapons in public. To the credit of the signatories, however, a national network of peace committees was in place. A budget and a bureaucracy to administer it had been established; big training, marketing, and advertising initiatives had been launched, numerous conflicts had been defused; and hundreds of rallies and marches had been monitored to help contain political violence.

But the stark reality was, that two years after the signing of the NPA, political violence was the cause of even more deaths than before, political intolerance remained a serious obstacle to stability, and poverty and deprivation had not been alleviated. The white right-wing parties were still refusing to sign the accord. The largest of the groups, the Conservative Party, was in fact calling on all "freedom-loving" people not to become involved in the "discredited" NPA.[83] The PAC, as well as the governments of three of the so-called independent states within South Africa, still refused to sign. The territories they administered therefore could not be targeted for the establishment of peace committees.

Did the NPA matter? Answers to this question will be sought in the sections that follow.

The drafters of the NPA recognized that if peace was to be achieved, the accord would have to go beyond the mere provision of conflict resolution mechanisms. It would also have to address some of the underlying structural causes of the violence, such as poverty, lack of proper policing, and the problems caused by an unrepresentative and authoritarian system of government. A holistic approach was adopted that was in effect aimed at changing South African society—a goal that goes beyond what one would normally expect from a peace accord. A reading of the NPA suggests that it had three main objectives: (1) *to eliminate political violence* by means of the network of RPCs and LPCs that would serve as peacemaking and peace-building mechanisms at the grassroots level; (2) *to promote democratization* by creating a climate of greater tolerance that would be more conducive to negotiations and the establishment of a multiparty democracy; (3) *to facilitate reconstruction and development*, specifically in those communities directly affected by the violence. The extent to which the NPA and its structures have managed to achieve these objectives provides an indication of their success or failure. The three objectives will therefore be my criteria for assessing the impact of the NPA.

5

IMPACT OF
THE NPA ON
DEMOCRATIZATION

A History Devoid of Democracy

Before assessing the NPA's effect on democratization, some of the inherently undemocratic constraints it had to contend with ought to be highlighted. The first relates to the absence from South Africa's history of any experience of democracy.

Before and during the apartheid era, black South Africans were excluded from decision making at all levels, and race discrimination was legally entrenched. The country had never experienced a proper democracy. The multiparty parliamentary system in which whites had taken part through regular elections resulted in a minority government that was by its very nature oppressive and that operated in isolation from the majority of the population. After 1990 there was a rapid dismantling of this system to make way for a proper democracy. This change toward a democracy was not merely a matter of negotiating a new constitution and other legal aspects; it required a fundamental change in the mindsets of all South Africans. A paradigm shift toward a different political culture was necessary if democracy was to gain ground in the country. This was a more formidable task than drawing up a new constitution. The political violence experienced both before and after February 1990 was an indication of how far South Africans were from toleration of those who supported different political parties. The country's history was devoid of any experience of political tolerance.

Apartheid was the ultimate expression of political intolerance toward those that were excluded because of their skin color. The ANC and the Communist Party, both of which had been banned and had operated from exile for more than two decades, developed very close links with the Soviet Union and other socialist states during that period. The PAC, also banned, developed links with Libya. The needs of a liberation struggle and the influence these countries had on the organizations were reflected in revolutionary policy positions and strategies adopted while in exile. The liberation struggle left little room for political tolerance. Strong hegemonistic tendencies manifested themselves within the ANC, and the notion that it spoke on behalf of "the people" meant that it automatically denied other organizations the same right.

The self-governing and independent states within South Africa had an abysmal record of democratic practices. Military rule (in the Transkei), effective one-party rule (in KwaZulu), and puppet governments manipulated by the South African government (in the Ciskei) were the order of the day.

When the signatories of the NPA committed themselves to uphold fundamental rights such as freedom of speech, peaceful assembly, and association, they must have realized that they were aiming very high, considering the realities on the ground. It would take a lot to change the undemocratic, intolerant, and oppressive political culture of the day to one in which political tolerance was practiced. South Africa had a long way to go before political pluralism was embraced by ordinary people.

A countrywide survey conducted during February 1993, eighteen months after the signing of the NPA, still found considerable resistance to democratic procedures and principles among all races in South Africa.[84] Among black, Asian, and colored future voters, there was a relatively widespread acceptance that other parties should not contest areas in which one party was dominant. Protest against other parties holding meetings was considered justified. The survey showed that five out of ten blacks rejected the right of formerly white parties to operate in black areas. These were some of the realities the NPA had to contend with.

"No-Go" Areas

The many "no-go" areas that existed were a constant reminder of the political intolerance that ordinary people had to contend with. These areas were to be found mainly in the Natal-KwaZulu Region and the Transvaal. No-go areas are townships or parts thereof, or significant rural areas, in which one political group has established a dominance or believes that it has done so and which supporters of that group then regard as closed to rival political groups. Attempts by rival political groups to canvass openly or to hold public meetings in no-go areas frequently result in physical clashes, violence, and killings. In the Natal-KwaZulu Region some townships and large tracts of rural areas are regarded as no-go areas for the ANC because of IFP dominance. Many deaths have resulted from attempts by the ANC to mobilize support or to hold marches or meetings in those areas.

In the same region, as well as in the Transvaal, many townships, some very large, are dominated by the ANC and are therefore regarded as no-go areas for the IFP or other political parties. Some predominantly ANC-supporting townships in the Transvaal tend to label all hostel dwellers as IFP supporters and so isolate them from community life. Hostel dwellers respond by regarding all township dwellers as hostile ANC supporters. Supporters of parties other than the ANC and the IFP are also affected. When the Democratic Party recently attempted to hold a public meeting in an ANC-dominated shack area south of Johannesburg, its supporters were attacked and attempts were made to set their cars on fire.

White right-wing parties also regard some of the areas in which they have significant support as closed to both de Klerk's National Party and the ANC. These are mainly rural areas of the Transvaal and the Orange Free State. Attempts have been made to prevent National Party public meetings from taking place, and ANC meetings have been disrupted. One recent example was an ANC meeting held on November 6, 1993, in the town hall of Middelburg, a middle-sized town in the Eastern Transvaal Region. The meeting was invaded by white right-wingers who forcibly broke it up and prevented it from continuing. According to the local Conservative member of Parliament, the action was their way of saying to the ANC "leave our town alone."[85] The *Sowetan* commented: "We have already seen the intolerance of the left of the political spectrum. Now the right is flexing its muscles."[86] When the ANC recently organized a protest march through the town of Brits, in the Northern Transvaal, the road into the town had to be cordoned off to enable the police to confiscate firearms that white right-wingers were threatening to bring in to stop the march. Heavily armed contingents of police with helicopters in the air were necessary to ensure that the march went off without violence. This experience has been repeated on many occasions in other areas.

The NPA code of conduct for political parties clearly prohibits the maintenance of no-go areas or any interference with free political activity.

Yet the unacceptable state of affairs has been allowed to continue. Political leaders occasionally exhort their supporters to allow free political activities by rival groups, but they seem to do so with the knowledge that little will be done about it by their supporters on the ground. The failure by political leaders to take disciplinary steps against supporters at the grassroots level has contributed to the general impression that the leadership will look the other way if incidents occur in no-go areas. The NPA structures have to contend with this reality.

Democratizing Role of Peace Structures

National Peace Committee

The NPA's effect on democratization has been most noticeable at the leadership level. Those senior political figures who were involved in negotiating the accord met with many of their counterparts from different political groups for the first time during that period. The entire exercise proved to be a trial run for the constitutional negotiations of December 1991, three months after the signing of the NPA. For example, during numerous meetings of the working groups that drafted the different chapters of the NPA, political opponents became acquainted with each other, created relationships, and built trust. The approximately 200 individuals involved in the working groups created a climate of constructive interaction that illustrated that multiparty negotiations were possible. Many of those involved in the working groups also participated in the subsequent constitutional negotiations. As John Hall, chairman of the NPC, has remarked, "The big thing that the Peace Accord did for negotiations was creating a network of people who knew each other. A lot of issues which were later to come up in the negotiations had already been discussed in the working groups."[87]

Even after the signing of the NPA, key political figures from all the signatory parties met on an ongoing basis as members of the NPC. The process that had preceded the signing had contributed to the stability the NPC experienced. When the multiparty constitutional negotiations collapsed in June 1992, after the Boipatong massacre,[88] the only multiparty forums at the national level that remained intact and through which different parties could communicate with each other were the NPC and the NPS. The peace structures therefore provided a neutral terrain for opposing political groups to meet during crises when other avenues of communication were difficult or impossible.

The limitations of the peace structures have, however, become more apparent as negotiations progress. While the NPC could weather the post-Boipatong CODESA crisis, it has not been able to escape all political crises. Since Mandela's reference to Buthelezi as a "surrogate of the South African government" during a speech at the United Nations in July 1992, the ensuing IFP-ANC tensions have made it impossible to convene a full meeting of the NPC attended by the leaders of the signatories. In accordance with the provisions of the accord, Buthelezi lodged a complaint with the NPC, alleging a contravention of the code of conduct for political parties. The NPC's inability to adjudicate this matter again highlighted one of the main weaknesses of the accord—its lack of teeth for dealing with alleged contraventions of the codes of conduct. The primary reason for this weakness was that the adjudicatory and enforcement procedures of the accord required multiparty consensus and cooperation. Even the decision to submit a dispute for adjudication or arbitration required a consensus in practice. In retrospect, an independent body would have had a much better chance of enforcing the agreed codes of conduct. Numerous complaints, lodged by a range of signatory parties, have piled up at the NPC without being settled. The enforcement mechanisms are clearly inadequate and need to be reinforced by amending the NPA. The provisions in the accord dealing with these aspects are vague and do not spell out how and by whom such adjudication, arbitration, or enforcement is to occur. Proposals in this regard have been finalized but they can only be put into effect with the approval of a full meeting of the NPC, preferably with the leaders of the various parties present. The fact that Buthelezi has on a number of occasions declined to attend has meant that the meetings could not be held and that a whole range of proposed amendments to the accord have been gathering dust. For more than eighteen months there has been a desperate need for all political leaders to jointly recommit themselves to the NPA and agree on mechanisms for strengthening it.

The NPC's inability to effectively adjudicate the complaint lodged by Buthelezi about Mandela's "surrogate" speech at the United Nations led Buthelezi to refuse to attend such a meeting of leaders of the signatories until the matter had been resolved. In addition, it was difficult to fix dates so that all the main political leaders were able to attend the same meeting.

The power play at the constitutional negotiations and the rise in the political temperature in anticipation of the April 1994 elections have resulted in the NPC struggling to function effectively. It has not received the commitment and backing from all political leaders that it needs to fulfill its task.

Regional Peace Committees

Members of the RPCs generally went through a more difficult adjustment period than was the case at the level of the NPC. They did not have the advantage of getting to know each other during a lengthy period before the formation of the committees. Particularly in the Natal-KwaZulu Region, where the violence is almost endemic, the RPC has found it difficult to isolate itself from the tensions and hatreds on the ground. The result is a fragile RPC that has been slower in making progress than most of the other ten RPCs. The Witwatersrand-Vaal RPC, on the other hand, has coped with major crises such as the assassination of Chris Hani and has managed to do so in a very creditable way. The establishment of a number of credible local peace structures and the effective joint planning and monitoring of political marches by monitors from peace structures as well as those from different political parties have given that RPC credibility and standing that have been widely recognized in the community. How much the democratization process has been enhanced as a result is again difficult to quantify. The result has certainly been positive but not as noticeable as at the national level. The cumulative impact of RPCs' activities in their regions can best be assessed by looking at the wide range of activities some of them engage in. The reports that regions submit to the NPS every two to three months provide an indication of the scope of their work. As an illustration, two such reports, one from a more successful region, the Western Cape RPC (Cape Town), and one from a committee that was struggling and experiencing debilitating internal problems, the Northern Transvaal RPC (Pretoria), are reproduced below. These reports cover the period of April and May 1993 and were submitted to a meeting with the NPS held on June 3, 1993. The verbatim report from the Western Cape RPC follows.

Report of the Western Cape Peace Committee
to the National Peace Secretariat
3–4 June 1993

1. Evaluation of the Program of the RPC

1.1 Support of the Political Process

The RPC has managed in the last two months to exert a greater influence on the political process on a regional level than before. Various meetings were held with the ANC and government structures and even with non-signatories to the Peace Accord, notably the PAC. The events following the assassination of Chris Hani, especially the outbreak of unprecedented violence in the centre of Cape Town, necessitated close cooperation with the various political bodies with the view to preventing a recurrence of what happened. We are happy to report that the various signatories are mutually supportive in these efforts.

The RPC can also report success in its efforts to influence policy on local government issues. One of these issues that has taken up a lot of RPC time is the Interim Measures Act.[89] Persistent violence has threatened or erupted in a growing number of communities in response to the implementation of the Act. The RPC has not only interceded locally, but also addressed the matter at the level of the Cape Provincial Administration, resulting in letters being circulated to the communities explaining the optional nature of the Act. Finally, a meeting with the Minister was held in which the views of the RPC were sympathetically received.

1.2 Crises Response

The major focus of the RPC has been crises response. This entails inter alia interventions and negotiations between Civic organisations and Municipalities, the South African Police [SAP] and Communities, Intergroup Conflicts and the monitoring of marches and meetings. Too many crises situations occurring at the same time and too little human resources are some of the biggest problems we encounter. The minutes of the RPC meetings reflect the amazing number of conflicts and disputes being dealt with by so few.

The education crisis has brought upon the RPC even more responsibilities. We consider it a breakthrough to already have had a meeting with COSAS [Congress of South African Students] and the promise of a future more structured relationship with this youth organization.

The violent crisis in the transport industry also needs special mentioning. The Western Cape RPC's Transport Subcommittee firefights when tensions escalate within the taxi industry often resulting in violent confrontations and killings. After extensive consultation and research the Subcommittee concluded that a major underlying cause of the conflict is the lack of integrated regional transport policy. The meeting of a Greater Metropolitan Transport Forum was facilitated and launched by the Subcommittee in March. A working Committee with representatives from taxi, civic leaders, transport experts and the police is now facing the task of sorting problems and seeking solutions again under the leadership of the RPC.

1.3 Training

The RPC has run two workshops on mediation and facilitation for the Executive Committee and a number of workshops for local committees. It has, however, been very frustrating that provision was not made for the training of secretariat staff. The need for staff training is essential to ensure effective mediation and intervention. It has become clear to the Western Cape RPC that, given the circumstances, our fieldworkers are more mediators and facilitators than anything else. To deny them basic training is very shortsighted.

2. South African Police–Community Relations

There has been a remarkable improvement in the relations between the SAP and communities in a number of towns where the RPC succeeded in facilitating workshops and meetings with the SAP.

The cooperation between the SAP and the organisations on the RPC is excellent. This is most gratifying in view of the strained relations that existed in the past between the SAP and many of these organisations represented on the RPC. In fact, cooperation on the level of the RPC is one of the outstanding features of the peace efforts in this region.

3. Media Department

3.1 Radio

Radio Xhosa has confirmed that the Peace Committee will take part in a bi-weekly phone-in education programme to talk about its work on the ground. The programme is aimed at the rural areas and at non-English-speaking Xhosa people living in the cities. We are currently looking for suitable Xhosa-speaking people from the various regions to participate in this programme. Radio Metro will also transmit information about the various Peace Committees, and needs the participation of English-speaking presenters.

3.2 Community Video Dialogues

The Media office in Cape Town will coordinate the radio programmes (with Marketing Committee) and provide a full script and information to presenters.

Video Dialogues is a series of 6–24 profiles of rural communities in transition, each focused around a particular conflictual issue (e.g., land rights, local government, educational reform, etc.) that is critical to the community, but has ramifications for many other communities across the country. The purpose is to create forums (with Local Peace Committees) to further public debate, dialogue and the management, if not resolution, of conflict within the communities. Community profiles around specific contentious issues will be screened within the communities themselves, as well as in public broadcast.

In documenting the debate/conflict in each community, two videos will be produced, using much of the same footage:

- A community video for use as a tool to mediate/open up debate, as well as educate/inform more broadly on an issue, within the community itself at a "town meeting" (and for use by other communities).

- A public broadcast video (to be shown on the South African Broad-casting Corporation) which profiles the community-in-conflict, but also includes footage from the "town meeting" at which the community video is screened/debated.

In this way, Video Dialogues will directly touch the people immedi-ately involved in the issue profiled, but also a much broader audience involved in similar social change, conflict and debate. We have an indi-cation of companies that are willing to give funding to the project (HR Trust, Warner Lambert and Echoing Green).

We need suggestions from each region of critical towns that can be covered. This project will then be coordinated with the RPC's in these regions.

3.3 Peace Education

Our office has received an offer from TSS (South African Broadcasting Corporation's learning channel) to provide them with a weekly 10-minute slot for school children on how to handle conflict, and issues relating to peace making and negotiations.

We have consulted with SACHED [South African Committee for Higher Education] and several other educational bodies and have a working group to finalise content of programmes. We need suggestions regarding content from other regions and possible schools from the regions to par-ticipate in the programme.

The report proceeds to list the six LPCs and three interim committees established in the region as well as the ten that were in the process of being established.

The impressive range of activities of the Western Cape RPC is bound to aid democratization in the region. The RPC was able to fulfill this function because it was representative and therefore had credibility and standing within the region. To a greater or lesser extent this also applied to the other ten RPCs in the country. Individual RPCs have, however, gone through their own crises for a range of reasons. The following extract from the report of the Northern Transvaal RPC to the same meeting in June 1993 provides an example of an RPC going through difficult times:

The Northern Transvaal Region therefore has on the whole the potential of widespread violence. I think it was the active monitoring of violence by especially the members of the executive representing the Alliance and the Civics together with the very active support by the two international observers that explains the measure of peace that still prevails in our region. This region wishes to emphasize the need to develop some form of remuneration for such monitors who literally day after day act at the instruction of and on behalf of the RPC as monitors all over the region wherever there is a need. They spend more time even than members attending meetings for whom we have already requested remuneration. The restrained and sensitive behavior of the S.A. Police particularly in mass demonstrations have also contributed a lot to our success as did the enthusiasm of other members of the RPC who are almost always available if called upon.

Internal Functioning of the Peace Committees

We are sad to have to report that within the RPC itself we had less success in the maintenance of peace. Personality clashes and deeply rooted distrust and insensitive behavior has often marred particularly the meetings of the RPC to the point that some participants lost interest. It is a serious situation that reduced the efficiency as well as the progress of the work of the RPC over a period of more than a year. One can only hope that it represents birth pangs of democratic interaction and that we will be able to grow out of the syndrome and save the peace structures for constructive action in the period of reconstruction that we hope we have entered in South Africa.

The local peace committees also reflect the political tensions of their surroundings and at times suffer from over-busy or dormant chairpersons who may have been nominated prematurely for a job that puts heavy demands on anyone. But they seem to have less internal strife than the Region.

Local Peace Committees

Throughout South Africa, RPCs and LPCs have gone through their own trials and tribulations with varying degrees of success. The fact that approximately 180 LPCs were in operation by October 1993, with more being established, means that in at least 180 local communities residents were for the very first time witnessing local leaders, sitting around the same table, who in the past would not have spoken to each other. In some areas no communication had existed between the IFP, the ANC, and other rival groups. Police and defense force members had not been able to establish normal communication channels with many black political activists in townships. To have community leaders, police, political groups, tribal chiefs, and church representatives jointly addressing community issues has never happened before. It has helped to create a measure of trust among members of the peace committees and show the communities that it is possible to work with "enemies" for the common good. Political tolerance and the notion of political pluralism is therefore being introduced by example into every community in which an LPC is established. How much this example actually affects communities is not measurable. The fact that most LPCs are able to operate, and that more are being established all the time, suggests that at worst they are being tolerated and at best they are successful and have community support.

The Commonwealth Observer Mission has described the NPA as a forum primarily for the reconciliation of South Africa's people: "One could cite numerous examples of how, albeit slowly and painfully, South Africans are getting to know each other through this Accord."[90] Although it is difficult to measure, the peace structures have made a positive contribution to democratization in local communities. This is recognized by many who justifiably point out that the impact could be greater if some of the weaknesses of the accord are addressed. One of the most consistent criticisms has been that the NPA was a top-down document that was implemented top-down and is therefore out of touch with community sentiments and needs.

The negotiations that led to the signing of the NPA were kept as confidential as possible for fear that the fragile process might collapse under the glare of publicity. For example, the five working groups charged with drafting the various chapters of the accord met behind closed doors, and the content of their discussions was not made public. The public in South Africa first learned of the content of the NPA on the day the signing ceremony took place. The NPA was widely welcomed, but it had been sprung on the average citizen without debate or input from the wider public. Millions of South Africans who live in rural areas or in townships or shack areas without electricity, or who are illiterate, have not even heard about the NPA. Most of those with television sets or radios soon learned that a peace accord existed but were not really aware of its content.

Political violence was more prevalent in poorer areas than in those where the households owned television sets. The awareness level of the NPA in many poor and violence-ridden areas was, and still is, low. Moreover, there was a long delay before the NPA text was available in the various indigenous languages, and the NPS marketing subcommittee chose to focus on a First World and more sophisticated target market rather than on ordinary people in the areas where the violence was occurring. These facts at least partly explain why the knowledge of, and support for, the NPA is far less pronounced at the grassroots than at the leadership level. It is clear that the peace structures, the political groups themselves, and the media have not done enough to inform people at the local level about the provisions of the NPA.

After a conference of member churches in July 1993, the SACC issued a sharp critique of the NPA that also referred to frustrations and problems at the local level. The points of criticism were preceded by a preamble that "notes with appreciation the sacrificial commitment of thousands of people working in the National Peace Accord structures across the land, through whose efforts numerous potentially violent situations have been peacefully negotiated." Referring to local communities, the SACC noted the following:

- There is a reluctance by grassroots communities involved in situations of violence to approach the NPA because of lack of confidence in the effectiveness of its witness protection programme.
- The dominant role of business in the NPA detracts from the participation and empowerment of the oppressed community.
- While wide publicity is given to the national structures of the NPA, insufficient resources are reaching the far more important regional and local Peace Committees who must deal daily with violence on the ground.
- Budgets and administration of finance are not sufficiently accountable to the people most affected by the violence.
- The virtual total exclusion of women from the structures.

The criticism of the witness protection program should not have been addressed to those involved with the NPA. The NPA has no mandate in this area because it is not provided for in the accord. The suggestion that the issue needs to be addressed is valid, as the lack of an effective witness protection program seriously undermines efforts to bring criminals to book. The other points raised by the SACC have substance and need to be addressed. A critical assessment is necessary, something that the NPS currently has under way. Everything possible must be done to ensure that LPCs and local communities are empowered to take responsibility for the peace process in their areas.

A number of critical evaluations of the NPA, and the operation of its structures, have been undertaken at both national and regional levels. Joint meetings between the NPS and chairpersons of the RPCs have been held to do that. The most independent and thorough evaluation thus far is one conducted over a five-week period in April and May 1993 by International Alert, an international nongovernmental alliance based in London.[91] At the invitation of the NPS, International Alert organized and cosponsored an evaluation of the peace structures and their operations by a group of international experts assisted by experts from South Africa.[92]

In a comprehensive report, the International Alert mission produced a "ground-breaking evaluation" that assessed the strengths and weaknesses of peace structures and recommended improvements.[93] With reference to grassroots support for the peace structures, the report states that

> there remains widespread public perception that the Accord and the Peace Structures are elitist in design and in implementation and have not adequately enlisted grassroots support. . . . The Peace Structures at the National and regional level remain dominated by relatively successful businessmen, lawyers, politicians and churchmen who are predominantly white and, almost invariably, speak no African language. Although some of these persons are extremely energetic and committed and can at times be effective in mediating between the political leadership and the security apparatus, they are limited in their ability to project the values and the procedures of the peace process to a wider constituency.

The task of giving grassroots structures a greater sense of ownership of the peace structures is complex. The lack of such ownership is the result of a number of factors, such as the content of the NPA, the way the accord was arrived at, the way some local structures were established, the race and class of some of those involved at regional and national levels, poor communication from the national to the grassroots levels, lack of resources, lack of expertise in taking charge, and lack of commitment and support from the political leadership. The fact that those immediately affected by the political violence are the communities at the grassroots level has meant that they have been preoccupied with local events and not with violence on a national scale. A successful initiative to form an NPA would therefore have come not from the grassroots level but rather, as indeed happened, from the national leaders who were concerning themselves with national issues. The NPA could only have happened as a result of an initiative by the elites. Perhaps wider consultation should have taken place in communities before establishing LPCs so that the communities could have been locked into the local peace structure from the outset. These and other points raised by critics are being addressed by the NPS and regional committees.

Despite these problems, however, the peace structures have made a significant contribution to democratization in South Africa. In its final report, the International Alert evaluation mission stated the following:

> Peace structures in a country undergoing a delicate period of transition must of necessity be imperfect. But in South Africa, the Peace Accord structure has made an invaluable contribution—in some instances making dialogue partners of those who before stood on opposite sides of the barricades. Where imperfect institutions of governance, justice and policing have been questioned, especially by the disadvantaged members of society, the peace structures have provided opportunities to allow people to articulate their grievances so that they can be more effectively redressed. In brief, although much more needs to be done, the Peace Accord structures have effectively broken ground. Nevertheless we cannot underestimate the limitations under which they operate, given the national political context.[94]

Role of International Observers

The arrival in 1992 of international observers from the United Nations, the European Community (EC), the Commonwealth, and the Organization of African Unity (OAU) helped make some no-go areas more accessible to other political groups. Their presence at rallies and marches with members of the peace committees had a sobering influence that often dampened the enthusiasm of political rivals for resorting to violence.

The international observers' arrival was precipitated by the massacre at Boipatong in June 1992. Forty-eight persons, most of them women and children, were killed when their shack settlement, south of Johannesburg, was attacked by men from nearby hostels. The incident caused shock and waves of protest throughout the country. The ANC suspended its participation in constitutional negotiations, and Mandela appealed to the United Nations to "find ways and means to normalize the deteriorating situation in South Africa and so try to resume the negotiations which have broken down."[95] In response UN secretary-general Boutros Boutros-Ghali sent former U.S. secretary of state Cyrus Vance to South Africa on a fact-finding trip. Vance received unprecedented cooperation from all political groups, including right-wing parties. He also met with members of the NPC, the NPS, and RPCs. From the political groups as well as the peace structures there was broad support for the suggestion that international observers be allowed to operate in South Africa, something the government had until then opposed.

Following the fact-finding mission, UN resolution 772 of August 17, 1992, was adopted authorizing the secretary-general to deploy UN observers in South Africa "in co-ordination with the structures under the National Peace Accord." The resolution further invited the secretary-general to assist in the strengthening of NPA structures and called on international organizations such as the OAU, the Commonwealth, and the EC to consider deploying their own observers in South Africa "in co-ordination with the United Nations and the structures set up under the Peace Accord."

At the end of July 1992 the first advance team of UN observers arrived in South Africa, followed over the next few months by additional UN observers as well as observer teams from the EC, the OAU, and the Commonwealth. They were deployed mainly in the violence-torn Natal-KwaZulu and Witwatersrand-Vaal Regions, with smaller teams stationed at other centers throughout the country. By September 1993, 61 UN, 9 Commonwealth, 15 EC, and 13 OAU observers had been deployed.

In accordance with their mandate, the international observers coordinate their activities with the RPCs and LPCs. They attend meetings of peace structures at all levels and communicate regularly with political groups across the spectrum. They are therefore kept informed about planned events such as political rallies and about potential conflicts. As the eyes and ears of the international community, their presence at such events has caused participants to show greater restraint. One rally that could have resulted in clashes and violence in the absence of international monitors was the large Shaka's Day rally addressed by Chief Minister Mangosuthu Buthelezi and Zulu king Goodwill Zwelithini in the KwaMashu township outside Durban in Natal on September 24, 1992. KwaMashu had been the scene of numerous clashes between supporters of the ANC and the IFP during the preceding years, leaving many dead and injured. By 1992, the township was generally regarded as an ANC stronghold, so it was virtually impossible for the IFP to meet and operate openly in the area. With the full cooperation and involvement of both the RPC (including the IFP, ANC, and police representatives), and international observers, a large rally, attended by approximately 23,000 people in the center of a tense KwaMashu, took place without any violence or deaths.

Although it is difficult to attribute the rally's success solely to the presence of international observers or RPC members, those who were present at the rally were almost unanimous in believing that the presence of the international observers played a major role. Not only did political opponents refrain from attacking each other, but the security forces were on their best behavior as well and conducted themselves in an impartial and professional manner. This certainly had not always happened in the past. The KwaMashu rally aptly illustrated that the presence of international observers and the active involvement of a peace committee could help create a climate in which free political activity could take place (even though the reason rivals did not attack each other was probably a fear of being identified by the international community and others as the aggressor, rather than a new-found conviction that free political activity ought to be allowed in KwaMashu).

Numerous examples similar to the KwaMashu experience can be cited throughout the country. Of course the presence of international observers and LPC and RPC members has not always prevented violence from erupting. But political marches, rallies, and meetings no longer constitute the same danger to life and limb in many areas as they did two years ago. Greater consultation between political groups and the authorities in planning the marches is one of the reasons for this improvement. In many areas, the peace committees have played a part in facilitating consultation. In April 1993, the chairman of the Goldstone Commission, Justice Goldstone, reported that more than 10,000 public marches had taken place throughout the country during the preceding eighteen months, most of them illegal, and that only 3 resulted in death or injury.[96] In some small white towns with right-wing administrations, marches by ANC supporters have taken place without incident, something that would not have happened two years ago.

Despite the continued existence of many no-go areas, and despite ongoing high levels of political intolerance, the peace structures, strengthened by the international observers, have helped spread the concepts of political pluralism and tolerance in South Africa.

Training of Peace Committees

The changing of a political culture and of attitudes will inevitably be a slow process. It can be accelerated and influenced through properly designed training programs. The entire South African population would probably benefit from a reeducation process that stresses reconciliation, respect for fellow human beings, tolerance, and democratic principles. Although in practice such an exercise is unlikely to materialize, a start has at least been made in the training of members of the peace structures.

The NPA provides for the training of LPC members "in conciliating disputes, running meetings, negotiating skills, etc." This is the responsibility of the NPS, which has established a training subcommittee to coordinate this function. Considerable resources and expertise have gone into training seminars for numerous LPCs and RPCs throughout the country. The seminars last one to three days and are conducted by paid professional trainers. By September 1993, 102 training workshops had been conducted, which means that well over 2,000 peace committee members have benefited from the training. Although training needs are different for every LPC, most training seminars deal with the content of the NPA, how to run meetings, mediation, facilitation, and negotiation, and generally with those skills that committee members may need to deal with the tasks in their area. Evaluation reports from participants often stress the importance of all the members of the peace committee being together at the same venue for the weekend.

If peace committee members are being equipped to resolve issues in their community through joint action with others from within the community, then the training seminars certainly advance the process of democratization. The empowerment of individuals and communities to take charge of issues that affect them and the ability to undertake joint initiatives for the benefit of the community as a whole constitute effective ways to counter violence. Training results are not immediately apparent, but they are an essential part of a process that leads to greater democratization.

For these training efforts to have a measurable national impact, however, they must reach a far wider audience than the 2,000 to 3,000 members of peace structures who have received training to date. In a total population of approximately 39 million, hundreds of thousands of individuals from all communities need to be equipped with basic skills for dealing constructively with conflict and developmental issues in their communities. The NPA structures could play a vital role in working toward this aim by providing the infrastructure through which all communities can be reached. For that to happen, however, ten times as many LPCs as the 180 that now exist must be established throughout the country.

Role of the Media

Not enough information about the activities of the LPCs and RPCs is available to the general public. More information would provide greater transparency and would help build trust in communities where peace committees exist and among the public at large. Peace structures need to be more proactive in making information available to the media and to peers within the communities, and the media need to reassess their poor track record in covering the peace structures. The drama of crowds, violence, and death makes for better headlines than the peaceful resolution of a dangerous conflict situation. For the media, the successes of peace structures often amount to non-events. An improvement has, however, taken place during 1993, as confirmed by the Commonwealth Observer Mission in its report to the Commonwealth Secretariat:

> Whereas when we first arrived, the Peace Accord structures received scant attention in the local media, now there is hardly an article on political tension in which the "thin orange line" of local monitors, in their luminous jackets and waving orange flags, is not mentioned. Indeed, one newspaper has gone so far as to assign a full time correspondent to covering the structures of the Peace Accord in the PWV region and elsewhere.[97]

6

THE NPA
AND
POLITICAL
VIOLENCE

Increase in Fatalities

Facts speak for themselves. The signing of the NPA did not result in a drop in the number of fatalities from political violence. There has been an upward trend during the two years since the accord was signed (figure 3), with a peak during July 1993, when 604 persons were killed.[98] During the year preceding the signing of the NPA (September 1, 1990, to August 31, 1991), 2,649 persons died. This figure increased to 3,404 during the year that followed the signing of the accord (September 1, 1991, to August 31, 1992). The figure for the following twelve months (ending August 31, 1993) was 3,567. What is noteworthy is that political violence remained concentrated in the two regions where the ANC-IFP rivalry is at its fiercest: the Natal-KwaZulu Region and the PWV area, which consists of the larger metropolitan areas of Johannesburg, Pretoria, and Vereeniging. While some deaths did occur in the rest of the country, the numbers are negligible in comparison with those in Natal and the PWV area. Figure 3 further illustrates that most of the country was only marginally affected by political violence, a fact that often goes unnoticed.

The NPA and its structures have therefore not succeeded in stemming or reducing political violence and resultant deaths. This has caused some, particularly those with high expectations, to become disillusioned with the accord. Resignation normally sets in after yet another shocking massacre or during a period when violence appears to be skyrocketing once more. During periods when peace structures clearly illustrate to the

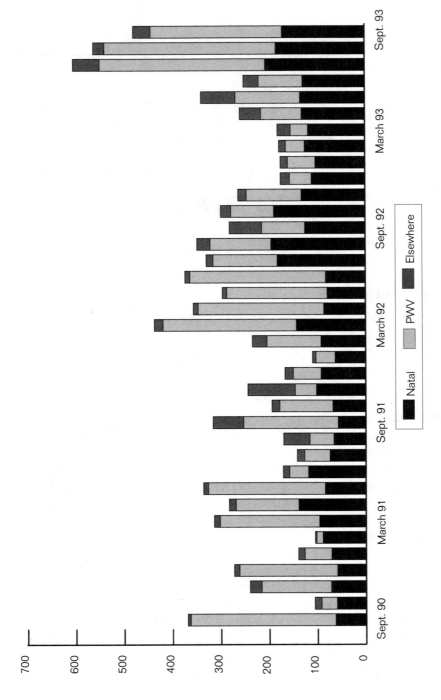

Figure 3. Politically related deaths, September 1990 through September 1993 (Human Rights Commission, Monthly Reports, Johannesburg)

public that they have helped defuse conflicts and save lives (e.g., after the Hani assassination), assessments of the NPA tend to become more balanced. After one of a series of massacres in the PWV area in June 1992, the daily newspaper with the largest readership in South Africa, the *Sowetan*, whose readers are mostly blacks, expressed its frustration by writing in an editorial that "the slaying of more than 30 people, coming so soon after those in Daveyton and Soweto, must be condemned in the strongest terms. It makes a mockery of the National Peace Accord. Frankly, the NPA is no longer worth the paper it is written on" (June 19, 1992).

The *Star*, published in Johannesburg, stated in an editorial on March 30, 1992: "We've said it before, but events force us to say it again. The National Peace Accord is manifestly not working, and that means people are still dying in the name of politics in South Africa. History demands from political leaders that they make it their responsibility to ensure that the sound structure created by the accord is translated into practical results." A few months later when the *Star* evaluated the NPA on its first anniversary, its conclusions were more measured:

> These figures [death statistics], depressing as they are, do not tell the whole story. At the very least the accord has brought together many disparate community leaders in local dispute resolution committees which are the basic structures of the whole peace initiative. These bodies have helped to keep the peace, even when they have been formed only after a terrible shedding of blood, as in Alexandria. Without an accord it would be easy for South Africa to be sucked up into a vortex of violence.[99]

In the absence of any objective standard (other than violence statistics) against which to measure the success or failure of the NPA, the tendency to rely solely on such statistics is understandable but inappropriate. This approach is partly a result of unrealistic expectations but is also due to a too-narrow interpretation of the objectives of the NPA— namely, a view that the sole objective was to reduce fatalities. A proper assessment of the NPA needs to take account of its broader objectives and the severe constraints under which the peace structures operate. These constraints limit what the peace structures can achieve. The report prepared by the International Alert evaluation mission acknowledges these limitations:

> The Accord is an imaginative document without real precedent in countries which continue to experience a high degree of political violence. However, it cannot be a substitute for political and constitutional reform. It must take as given the imperfections and inadequacies of the political

system and its history of violence. The Accord can therefore at best address some of the symptoms of political violence, but it cannot overcome the structural causes of violence.[100]

One of the structural causes of violence that directly affects LPCs' ability to resolve conflicts and create peace relates to the crisis of governance that black townships in South Africa have been experiencing for many years. Unrepresentative and corrupt local rule and the fact that the government has never been answerable to a black electorate have resulted in an absence of viable formal authority in the townships and therefore a lack of proper government in black communities. In democratic societies central government, local authorities, the courts, and the police provide meaningful avenues for people to raise their grievances and settle disputes. In South African townships these institutions, where they exist, frequently lack the will, the legitimacy, and the capacity to do so. In such circumstances it is inevitable that minor disputes escalate into major confrontations and resorting to violence becomes commonplace. The NPA structures may mitigate these trends, but they cannot resolve the crisis of governance or become substitutes for the police, the courts, and the government.[101]

Changes in Patterns of Violence

The nature of the violence has also changed during the past two to three years. What has become more prevalent is not only assassinations[102] and killers running amok on trains, but also larger-scale massacres of apparently innocent and defenseless people. Anthony Minnaar defines a massacre as an event in which five or more persons are killed in a single attack by one group of attackers only.[103] Before 1990, massacres were usually a result of security force action during strikes or political protests. From 1990 on, massacres have occurred to an increasing extent in those communities that have been most severely affected by the ongoing violence—Natal and the Transvaal. Figure 4 illustrates the increasing number of fatalities resulting from massacres in these two regions. Very few massacres have occurred elsewhere in South Africa.

Most attackers remain unidentified and "unknown" despite large awards offered by the police. Political parties do not claim responsibility. The involvement of a "third force," intent on fanning violence for its own political aims, has been suspected, but no conclusive evidence has come to light to confirm such claims. The peace structures stand helpless

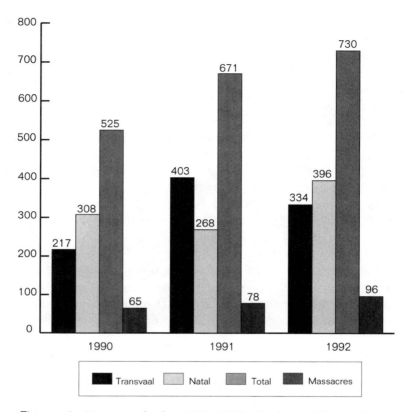

Figure 4. Massacre deaths, 1990–1992 (Anthony Minnar, Trevar Keith, and Sam Pretorius, *An Analysis of Massacres in South Africa, 1990–1992* (Centre for Conflict Analysis, Human Sciences Research Council, Pretoria, 1993)

in the face of this form of violence. These massacres cause great insta-bility and fear in strife-torn communities, and many local inhabitants lose faith in the ability of NPA structures to create peace.

A factor that has also changed the nature of the violence has been the proliferation of illegal firearms. Members of various political groups, crime syndicates, and ordinary criminals are involved in smuggling thousands of illegal firearms. Military sources have estimated that in 1991, 1.5 million AK-47 assault rifles were unaccounted for in neigh-boring Mozambique. Although the price for these rifles varies, crime syndicates commonly exchange a bag or two of cornmeal (worth about

R50 or $15) for an AK-47 from starving guerrilla fighters.[104] The effect of the illegal arms trade on the violence in South Africa is that the number of deaths and injuries per incident has increased.

Role of Peace Structures in Limiting Violence

Despite shortcomings of the NPA and the constraints under which it operates, LPCs in many areas have made a substantial difference in their communities.[105] Committees have successfully dealt with many local issues that could have resulted in violence including taxi wars in the Western Cape Region, consumer boycotts in the Northern and Eastern Transvaal Regions, squatter issues and hospital strikes in the Orange Free State and in the Transvaal, civic municipal disagreements, church disputes, opposition to rate increases, disputes over grazing rights for cattle, and many protest marches and other political gatherings throughout the country.

The most dramatic intervention in a potentially explosive situation occurred when the Witwatersrand-Vaal RPC played a decisive role in containing political violence in the Johannesburg area after the Chris Hani assassination, which occurred on April 10, 1993. Only weeks before his death, an opinion poll had ranked Hani the second most popular leader in South Africa (after Mandela). In Johannesburg up to 200,000 people attended Hani's funeral, which was divided between a soccer stadium and the Boksburg cemetery, 28 miles (45 km) away. The RPC, with the involvement of the ANC, the South African Police, and others who serve on the committee, jointly worked out a strategy to monitor and control the large and volatile crowds. The RPC, the ANC, and COSATU mobilized 240 volunteers to act as peace monitors. A communications network, linking all 240 monitors by radio, was set up. Joint operational centers, staffed by police, ANC representatives, and members of peace structures, were established. The police or monitors at the scene advised these centers by radio of potential trouble spots so that marshals and political leaders on the spot could first try to mediate a solution before the police were asked to move in. Agreement had to be reached about routes for the marchers, location of police reserve forces, and other operational matters. Although some deaths did occur, and houses and vehicles were burned, there was a consensus by those involved on the day that the regional peace structure had helped contain the violence and destruction and prevent a disastrous escalation of violence.

In other parts of the country many peace structures helped limit violence during hundreds of protest marches and memorial services. Their efforts often went unnoticed. They performed their task without being under the local and international spotlight and under less dramatic circumstances than those in large cities like Durban, Cape Town, or Johannesburg. Their successes were not recorded or publicized, but they have made a difference in the communities where they operate.

The NPA therefore does matter. It has made a difference. It has been instrumental in containing violence to levels that would otherwise have reached even more alarming heights.

7

ROLE OF THE NPA IN RECONSTRUCTION AND DEVELOPMENT

Poverty and Political Violence

It is generally accepted that the poor socioeconomic conditions under which most black South Africans live have contributed to raising the level of violence. Poverty and a fierce competition for resources occur in all areas where political violence is experienced. Some regard poverty, unemployment, and the lack of proper housing and basic services as the primary causes of political violence.[106] The Goldstone Commission, investigating the November 1992 violence in Tokoza, a township near Johannesburg, found that while political rivalry triggered violence in the impoverished townships, the socioeconomic conditions in those areas were its primary cause.

Although poverty and economic decline do contribute to heightened frustrations, tensions, crime, and greater lawlessness, what pushes people over the threshold to "violent behavior which is intended in some way to influence the political process"—that is, political violence—is mainly intense political competition. Poverty is therefore an important contributory factor, but insufficient evidence exists to suggest that it is the primary cause. In many areas outside the Transvaal and Natal, poverty is at least as bad as that in those two provinces. An example is the vast, overcrowded shack areas around Port Elizabeth in the Eastern Cape Region, where one of the highest unemployment rates in the country can be found. The Port Elizabeth metropolitan area is regarded as one of the two fastest-growing areas in the country, the other being the Cape Town metropolitan area.[107] The Port Elizabeth area has always been regarded as highly politicized, with strong support for the liberation movements. Living conditions for the hundreds of thousands of black residents are probably worse than in most townships around Johannesburg and Pietermaritzburg in Natal. Yet, for the past three to four years, political violence has not been a serious problem. During the 1980s the Port Elizabeth area was one of the centers of resistance against the government and its structures. Many lives were lost through harsh clampdowns by the security forces, "necklace" killings (in which tires were placed around victims' necks and set on fire), and factional clashes. Since February 1990, however, the area has been relatively calm and stable.

Figure 3 also gives an indication of the relatively low incidence of deaths from political violence in areas other than Natal and the PWV area. In those relatively violence-free areas the competition for resources is as intense as it is in Natal and the PWV area. Political violence therefore occurs not primarily in areas where poverty and deprivation are widespread, but in areas where poverty and poor socioeconomic conditions combine with intense political rivalry, particularly between the ANC and the IFP. Such rivalry does not exist, for example, in the Port Elizabeth area, where the IFP is inactive and the ANC predominates. It could be argued that ANC political control in the area prevents the entry of other political groups, but that would still not explain why the poverty and poor living conditions in surrounding townships and shack dwellings have not sparked large-scale conflicts between rival factions or between those who compete for the scarce resources.

Trade Union Influence

Whether or not they believed that poverty was the primary cause of political violence, those who drafted chapter 5 of the NPA certainly appreciated the importance of poverty as a contributing factor. Socioeconomic development could defuse some of the tensions, and it was therefore envisaged that the NPA should play a role in facilitating it. The emphasis was on facilitation and not on becoming the main vehicle for it. Development was to take place primarily in communities at the grassroots level, particularly in areas affected by political violence. Working Group 3, established by the preparatory committee after the June 22, 1991, peace meeting to draft recommendations relating to reconstruction and development, had prominent trade unionists as members.

They ensured that this aspect received the necessary attention. They had better insight into the harsh conditions at the grassroots level than most politicians, black or white. Mike Morris and Doug Hindson, who have close links with the trade union movement, emphasize the broad social, economic, and political forces in play when analyzing and seeking solutions to political violence. Great emphasis is placed on the importance of redistributing resources as an integral element of addressing violence: "To succeed, negotiations over violence in the black residential areas need to be part of the renegotiation of a whole city and its resources. Equally, negotiations over violence nationally need to be part of the renegotiation of the nation's resources and how they are deployed."[108] Morris and Hindson are critical of what they describe as the present "neo-liberal" approach to development, which is primarily growth oriented and tends to accentuate class differences, not only between black and white, but also among blacks. These growing class differences perpetuate tensions and antagonism in black areas. A reconstruction course that narrows class differences and addresses the social and economic imbalances is necessary; otherwise "new social and economic fault lines will reassert themselves with a vengeance."

The NPA's strong emphasis on grassroots empowerment and the involvement of local communities in the development process was primarily due to the influence of trade union members. The thinking of Morris and Hindson reflects that of many key individuals in COSATU. They felt that the approach to development in black communities was in need of drastic changes and hoped that the NPA would clear the way for such new approaches.

Has the NPA made an impact in that regard? Just as those who were intensely involved with the peace process were disappointed when political leaders turned their attention away from the NPA toward constitutional negotiations, so must those who had a keen interest in development have been disappointed by the lack of interest and commitment shown to that aspect of the accord by both politicians and the business community.

Role of National and Regional Subcommittees

Chapter 5 of the accord provided for the NPC and the RPCs to establish permanent subcommittees for socioeconomic reconstruction and development. These, particularly at the regional level, were slow in the making.

There was a lack of clarity in the NPA as to who would fund these committees and how they would fit in with other structures of the NPA.
John Hall, chairperson of the NPC, appointed Warwick Barnes, a person from the private sector with many years of experience in the field of
development, to head the National Subcommittee for Socioeconomic
Reconstruction and Development. This subcommittee had the task of
first defining its role, of identifying sources for funds, and of establishing
links with RPCs and LPCs. Existing development organizations had to
be persuaded that their development role would not be threatened, and
the government was asked to demonstrate its commitment by making a
financial contribution. A sum of R5 million ($1.5 million) was made
available to a fund established by the subcommittee, and facilities to
draw on another R5 million were provided. For every donation procured
on behalf of chapter 5 activities, the subcommittee would be able to
draw on the funds provided by government on a one-to-one basis. This
process was geared toward encouraging the private sector, development
agencies, and international governments to support the development
activities of the NPA. The funds received from nongovernment sources
were negligible.

Problems were experienced in establishing regional subcommittees,
and only some of the eleven regions had established active subcommittees by the end of 1993. It was virtually impossible to begin working at
the local level until regional subcommittees were in place. As recently as
June 1993, Barnes reported that "a positive momentum has developed
both with regard to the structuring of the Socio-economic Reconstruction
and Development Committee and the appointment of co-ordinators in
each region. The process has, however, been frustrated by the understandable preoccupation by Chairpersons with the violence, particularly over the last two months."[109]

A few small reconstruction and development projects were, however,
successfully undertaken. The most notable was aimed at a rural area
near the coastal town of Port Shepstone in Natal. Between 1990 and
1992, violent clashes had taken place between ANC-supporting youth
and IFP-supporting groups led by local tribal chiefs. Hundreds of youths
were driven out of the area to become refugees, scores of houses were
burned, and many people lost their lives. With the involvement of the
LPC in Port Shepstone, assisted by members of the Commonwealth
Observer Mission, a truce was negotiated after many meetings held
toward the end of 1992. The agreement provided, among other things,

that refugees would be allowed to return and that attempts would be made to repair damaged properties. ANC and IFP representatives jointly prepared an inventory that identified 281 householders who required assistance to repair well over 560 rooms. The National Sub-committee for Socioeconomic Reconstruction and Development approved a budget of R663,000 ($197,000) to cover the estimated cost of repair and appointed a project coordinator to oversee the task. While some tensions remain in the area, there has been a significant reduction of political violence from what was experienced between 1990 and 1992.

Some successful but isolated reconstruction activities have therefore been undertaken, but these are negligible in comparison with what the drafters of chapter 5 envisaged. They are insufficient to make a notice-able impact at the regional or national level. In a speech delivered on May 11, 1993, Angela King, the chief of mission of the UN Observer Mission in South Africa, referred to the lack of progress in this regard: "We also deplore that few practical measures have been taken to give effect to the Accord's provisions on socio-economic reconstruction and development."[110]

More recently, and in line with the recommendations of the Inter-national Alert evaluation mission, a fundamental restructuring of the national subcommittee, its role, and that of RPCs has been initiated by the NPC and the NPS. Socioeconomic reconstruction activities in the future are likely to be more closely integrated into the activities of RPCs and LPCs to ensure that they become more accountable and transparent. Lack of funding, a preoccupation by committees with violence crisis management, and a lack of commitment from political parties and the business community will, however, continue to hamper the socioeco-nomic reconstruction and development activities of the peace structures. As South Africa moves closer to a newly elected national government, a new development policy may be created. Until that has been finalized in many areas, the existing peace structures will continue to be the only representative and neutral local structures through which local devel-opment can be channeled.

8

CONCLUDING COMMENTS
The NPA in Perspective

At the beginning of 1990, a confluence of national and international developments and the presence of exceptional political leadership made it possible to embark on a peace process during a volatile and violence-ridden transition from apartheid to democracy:

- The collapse of the Soviet Union ended the Cold War and the rivalry between the superpowers in Africa. The "Russian threat," as the South African government had perceived it, was no more. Space was now available for the new leader of the governing party, F. W. de Klerk, to take imaginative steps of reform.
- International pressure on the South African government had reached a critical stage.
- The growing internal revolt of the 1980s against apartheid had gained a momentum that could no longer be effectively addressed through firm security action.
- The ANC in exile came to the realization that the "armed struggle" had failed to make any major dents in the armor of the South African government and was therefore not going to deliver a political victory.
- Nelson Mandela had taken the initiative from prison to prepare for negotiations.
- Two exceptional leaders, Mandela and de Klerk, happened to have leadership positions at this crucial time in South Africa's history. Despite twenty-seven years in prison, Mandela called for reconciliation,

peace, and unity. De Klerk steered his party onto a radically different course, allowed free political activity, called for equal rights, and proposed negotiations for a new nonracial and democratic constitution. The two leaders had obvious political differences, but there was much common ground in their vision of a new South Africa.

The process of fundamentally transforming the political and social system was driven by South Africans without the involvement of an outside third party. This made it unnecessary for political leaders to communicate through third-party channels and led to the establishment of direct lines of communication between South Africa's divergent political leadership. The minimum level of trust and understanding necessary to embark on a process of negotiations could therefore be established through a natural process of direct communication rather than through intermediaries.

The release of political leaders and the unbanning of organizations at the beginning of 1990 led to the paradoxical phenomenon that political violence aimed at the white minority government and its structures decreased significantly while black factional violence rocketed to unprecedented levels. The liberalization of coercive apartheid laws and the lifting of restrictions on political activity were not sufficient to create a climate conducive to negotiations. The growing spiral of political violence increasingly prevented political groups from focusing on constitutional negotiations and caused growing political tensions and polarization among ordinary people.

By the beginning of 1991 all the political groups who were keen to start negotiations saw violence as the most serious obstacle to negotiations. The self-interest of every major political group was being undermined by one common problem, political violence. The conditions therefore existed for all those political groups, despite their divergent political agendas, to cooperate in pursuit of a common objective—to address violence and achieve peace so that constitutional negotiations could commence. This distinguishes South Africa's situation from that in which most other conflict-ridden societies find themselves when peace initiatives are contemplated. As long as rival or warring factions do not perceive the pursuit of peace as being in their own self interest, attempts to make peace remain highly problematic. Peacekeeping through military or other intervention may appear possible, but if peacemaking is to follow, warring factions have to be persuaded that the conflict is against their own self-interest and that compromise will be necessary to prevent further harm to that interest.

Although the ANC, the IFP, the South African government, and others realized that a joint peace effort was required, none of the political leaders was in a position to facilitate a peace agreement because of distrust and suspicions about political agendas. Moreover, some leaders feared that supporters would interpret an initiative to mediate as a sign of weakness. Leaders from civil society, through a joint initiative between the churches and organized business, became the successful mediators and succeeded in facilitating a National Peace Accord that can justifiably be called unique. Because some components of South Africa's civil society were active and well organized, it was possible to rely on indigenous mediators to both persuade and pressure the main actors to come to terms. The absence of strong civil society structures in countries in which national conflicts result in violence—for example, Angola—makes it more difficult to resolve the conflict domestically and tends to lead to a dependence on outside third-party mediators.

The signing of the NPA on September 14, 1991, proved to be the catalyst that brought the leaders of all political groups (with the exception of three white right-wing groups) together in one room for the first time. Even more important was the fact that they all endorsed the content of the accord. Agreement now existed about some of the basic principles that would apply during and beyond the transition. The first broad outlines of the new South Africa were established. The goal was a multiparty democracy in which equal rights and fundamental freedoms would be respected and upheld. Norms of political conduct during the transition were now set, and a joint effort would be launched to address the violence. As the International Alert evaluation mission concluded, "Its [the accord's] significant success lies in developing a 'peace culture,' in securing an ideological commitment from the principal political actors to 'political tolerance,' and in being able to establish procedures and mechanisms for crisis management."[111]

The signing of the accord was a result of a diverse political elite deciding to enter into a pact to pursue mutually beneficial objectives. The enormous task awaiting those who were to implement the accord was to work for the same degree of consensus among ordinary supporters that the elites had reached at the national level.

The issue of political violence having been addressed through the NPA, the elites were ready to move on to the next main objective, the negotiations for a new constitution. The NPA's implementation did not enjoy the same priority as its creation. Senior representatives from the signatory parties were nevertheless designated to pursue this task.

Antagonism and divisions at regional and community levels made the establishment of a countrywide network of RPCs and LPCs a time-consuming and often difficult task. The accord had been designed by leaders without the involvement of their support bases, it was implemented from the top down, and people at the grassroots level were not properly briefed, either through their political parties or through the media, about the content and objectives of the accord. Despite these and other flaws, an expanding countrywide network of 11 RPCs and 180 LPCs was in place two years after the signing. Some 8,000 volunteers, representing a wide range of political and interest groups, were active in peace committees.

Political violence did not decline after the signing of the accord—it increased. In many communities, often those in violence-torn areas, peace committees had not yet been established. Some white right-wing parties, the PAC, and AZAPO were still not signatories, although individual supporters of the Conservative Party and the PAC were active in some of the structures. Despite many flaws and constraints, the accord has made an invaluable contribution to paving the way for constitutional negotiations and creating a climate that eased the transition from apartheid rule to a new democracy:

- It has helped contain political violence to levels that would otherwise have been even worse.
- It has contributed to democratization by bringing together, through the nationwide network of peace committees, political opponents and representatives from a wide range of interest groups to jointly promote peace, political tolerance, mutual understanding, and the building of trust.
- It has provided neutral forums through which issues relating to reconstruction and development, local government, transport, services, and police-community relations could be addressed jointly at the grassroots level.

In the deeply divided society of South Africa, which many predicted would head toward a destructive racial war, the NPA represents a brave and historic attempt to build new sources of legitimacy and to begin to restructure society by getting political parties and organizations to agree on basic principles of democracy, codes of conduct for political parties and security forces, and procedures and mechanisms for resolving conflicts peacefully.

EPILOGUE

The Last Leg: Toward Elections for a New Government

Previous chapters in this book covered the first two years of the existence of the NPA, September 1991 to September 1993. The unimaginable has since happened. The first nonracial democratic elections took place peacefully at the end of April 1994. The election was declared substantially free and fair, the result was accepted,[112] and a new government of national unity has assumed office with Mandela as president. This epilogue is written two weeks after the elections, with the new cabinet just having been appointed and South Africa still in a buoyant mood.

The months leading up to the elections from September 1993 were ones of great uncertainty. Anxiety existed as to whether the elections would be able to take place as scheduled at the end of April 1994. Delays in the negotiating process had resulted in a late start for those transitional structures that were designed to level the playing field before the election and those that were to organize and run the elections. The Transitional Executive Council (TEC), for example, held its first meeting on December 7, 1993. This council and its substructures consisted of representatives from different political parties who assumed significant powers during the remainder of the preelection transition. It effectively ended forty-five years of executive National Party rule. Under the statute that governed its actions, the TEC and its subcouncils exercised many executive powers in the areas of finance, policing, defense, intelligence, and local government. To prepare for the election with such a late start seemed a formidable task.

The Independent Electoral Commission (IEC), an independent body established by the multiparty negotiating forum to organize and run the election, had an equally late start. While major voter education initiatives were under way, significant sections of the population were totally unaware that an election was in the offing. In a nationwide survey conducted during November 1993, nearly 20 percent of those questioned had no idea that the election would take place.[113]

There was concern that the campaign and the election days themselves could degenerate into uncontrollable violence and conflict. In an attempt to deal with anticipated election-related violence, the peace structures geared themselves to train thousands of peace monitors. In addition, political parties such as the ANC, the IFP, and the National Party sent some of their supporters to workshops run by the peace structures to be trained as marshals. The objective was to provide political parties with their own trained marshals who would control crowds at political rallies and processions. Thirty-three workshops were held to train more than 2,800 marshals.

The major political parties embarked on their election campaigns with large rallies, accompanied by the usual robust rhetoric to be expected during such a crucial scramble for political power. Buthelezi, playing a game of tactical brinkmanship and saber rattling, refused to participate in any of the transitional structures. What caused even more concern was his constant threat that the IFP would not participate in the coming elections unless certain conditions, such as greater regional autonomy, were met. The Zulu king, Goodwill Zwelithini, entered the fray with growing demands that the interim constitution should accommodate a Zulu monarchy. Some predicted that a free and fair election was not possible in the Natal-KwaZulu Region unless the IFP participated and the king's demands were met.

White right-wing groups, who rejected the new interim constitution and refused to be part of the TEC, demanded a confederation and constitutional provisions for a "Volkstaat" (white Afrikaner homeland) for Afrikaners. Growing threats of violence and civil war emanated from these quarters. In the provinces of the Transvaal and the Orange Free State, more than thirty bomb and sabotage attacks took place, the most dramatic ones being a bomb explosion on April 25 at a taxi rank in Germiston, a town near Johannesburg, in which ten persons were killed and forty-one injured, and a car bomb at Jan Smuts Airport near Johannesburg on April 27, the second election day, which injured twenty-one. In the Johannesburg vicinity alone, bombings during the leading up to the elections killed 21 persons and injured nearly 200.[114] Thirty-four members of the right-wing Afrikaner Weerstandsbeweging were arrested following these attacks.

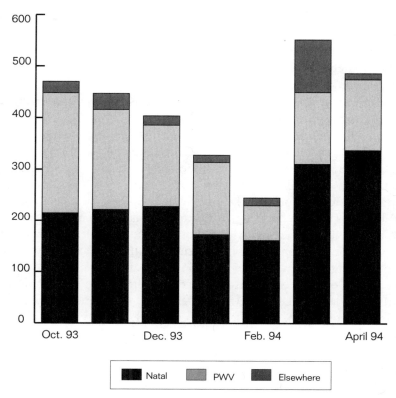

Figure 5. Politically related deaths, October 1993 through April 1994 (Human Rights Commission, Monthly Reports, Johannesburg)

The political temperature was therefore rising as the election campaigns intensified. This rise in the political temperature, however, did not translate into an overall increase in political violence or deaths. Since July 1993, when deaths from political violence peaked, successive monthly declines in the death figures had taken place—a most encouraging development. Shortly before the election, however, a serious escalation of political violence suddenly occurred. March and April 1994 recorded levels of political violence not experienced since the middle of 1993. During March alone 552 persons died as a result of the political violence—an average of nearly 18 a day (figures 3 and 5).[115]

Three events contributed significantly to the high death toll: the uprising in the former independent state of Bophuthatswana, attacks on the mass march by IFP-supporting Zulu royalists near the ANC head office in Johannesburg, and countrywide prison strikes and riots demanding the franchise for prisoners. These events resulted in 120 deaths—approximately 22 percent of the total for March. The March death toll also included eleven persons killed in a massacre near Durban in Natal, twenty killed as a result of security force actions (mainly in Bophuthatswana), and five lives lost in taxi conflicts.

In Natal, political violence rose sharply during March. Both IFP and ANC supporters openly flaunted automatic firearms at rallies, and free political activity become virtually impossible in many areas because of intimidation and violence. On March 31, President de Klerk declared a state of emergency for the whole of Natal-KwaZulu. Buthelezi and the IFP kept up their defiant nonparticipation, making it difficult for the IEC to plan for the election within those areas under the jurisdiction of the KwaZulu homeland. Political violence continued into April with the state of emergency having only a marginal impact. One death that caused exceptional outrage was that of a peace monitor who was killed near Durban in Natal. The South African Defence Forces were deployed, but in insufficient numbers to effectively cover all flash point areas in the region. Inaccessible areas and hilly terrain added to their problems.

On April 19, one week before the elections were due, Buthelezi suddenly announced the IFP's full participation. The country breathed a sign of relief. Last-minute agreement had been reached between the government, the ANC, and the IFP that the constitution would be amended to provide for a Zulu monarchy in the Natal-KwaZulu Region. Political violence started to subside in Natal and the rest of the country but nevertheless continued until the actual voting days arrived. The unexpected and almost eerie absence of political violence and death during those four days (except for the Jan Smuts Airport car bomb) caught everyone by surprise. The four voting days were the most peaceful, violence-free days for years. Not only was there no violence and a massive drop in ordinary crime, but the cooperation and goodwill that was exhibited between South Africans from across the spectrum created a new sense of national unity and optimism for the future.

The peace structures continued to play an important role during the preelection months, albeit with an emphasis different from that of the past. During the months before the election, the conditions under which the peace structures operated changed fundamentally. The establishment of the TEC and the IEC meant that for the first time legitimate representative structures with real decision-making powers were in place. It was the absence of such legitimate authority structures and the absence of communication channels between the contesting groups in the political arena that contributed to the establishment of the NPA in 1991. By the end of 1993 such structures were established in the form of the TEC and IEC, which overshadowed the peace structures. The TEC and IEC were equipped to deal with numerous conflicts as well as with complaints that arose from the conduct of supporters from different political parties. The IEC had adopted a code of conduct for political parties that largely overlapped that contained in the NPA. But the IEC had greater success in adjudicating complaints than the NPC. Unlike the NPC, the IEC did not suffer from the constraint of having to rely on multiparty consensus; it had legal authority and could enforce its decisions and rulings. The IEC established an independent structure under its auspices to enforce the agreed code of conduct and impose tough fines and penalties. In Natal the IFP received a stiff fine for occupying a stadium in advance of a planned ANC rally. In Cape Province the IEC forced the National Party to withdraw an election pamphlet that exploited racial differences, and in the Transvaal the ANC was fined when one of its supporters hurled a stone at de Klerk.

Public attention was therefore focused more on the election-related activities of the TEC and the IEC than on the activities of the peace structures. A historic election campaign was under way, and it is understandable that the drama and tensions that accompany such a campaign received more prominence. What had not changed, however, were the numerous disputes and conflicts at grassroots level that were unrelated to the election campaign. This is where the by then more than 250 LPCs continued to do invaluable work. Just as they had during the two previous years, the LPCs successfully dealt with numerous conflicts, thereby helping to contain political violence, promoting the democratization process, and generally helping create a climate in which an election campaign was possible.

A major contribution by the peace structures to the peaceful holding of elections was the provision of almost 13,000 trained peace monitors. Between the beginning of February 1994 and April 25, the day before the election, the training units of the peace structures conducted 456 workshops and trained 12,577 peace monitors throughout the country. The monitors were volunteers selected from within the various communities. During voting days they were on duty in and around polling stations as

well as at assembly points where a potential for conflict existed. Wearing
their distinctive orange peace accord jackets and armbands, they received
praise from the IEC and all political parties for the role they played and
the way they conducted themselves as politically neutral monitors. Even
at the inauguration of President Mandela, peace monitors with their
distinctive flags, and peace emblems of two doves in a circle, were visible at the point where all foreign dignitaries emerged from their motor
vehicles to attend the function. The funding that made such a major
training operation possible was obtained from the British government
via the Overseas Development Agency.

Future of the Peace Structures

During the two and a half years of the NPA's existence, the peace structures have played a vital role in holding together the fabric of society at
a time when no other institution had the legitimacy or capacity to do
so.[116] Now a popularly elected government exists. The nine new provinces
in South Africa have each elected a regional government that can address
regional issues with a legitimacy not possible under previous administrations. Within the next year, local government institutions will be restruc-
tured, followed by local elections. Does the NPA have a role under these
changed circumstances?

The debate about the future of the peace structures is presently under
way within the peace structures themselves. Those who have recently
been elected to powerful positions in government are still finding their
feet and are, at this stage, occupied with urgent national issues of reconstruction. A fear exists that they may now regard the NPA and existing
peace structures as superfluous because the NPA was designed primarily
to span the period up to the election of a new legitimate government.
The new authorities may believe government structures are now equipped
to effectively pursue the objectives of the NPA.

It is probably correct that in any normal, stable democracy, many of
the functions presently fulfilled by the peace structures are handled by
the legitimate structures and institutions within society. Community
conflicts, reconstruction, and development, as well as local government
issues, are normally the domain of courts, police, social and economic
policy programs, and the various democratically elected organs of government. Some believe that the situation in South Africa is now normal
enough that the country can follow such a route. Such an assessment

is, however, unrealistic. While at the national level normality may have arrived in that an elected government exists that will operate within the limits of the new constitution, at the local level most of the factors responsible for conflict in the past remain and will remain for some time to come.

South Africa remains a deeply divided plural society with significant racial, religious, ethnic, class, and linguistic divisions. The modernization to which large sections of the population have been subjected will continue for a few decades. The political transition, which has brought heightened expectations for the majority and greater fear and anxiety for minorities, has not ended because of the election. The combined consequences of pluralism, modernization, and transition will therefore continue to threaten South Africa's stability. The fact that the new interim constitution provides for a government of national unity and for a five-year period of power sharing between the main political groups illustrates that political leaders recognize the potential for instability. Maximum effort, including the contribution by peace structures, will be required to firm up the fragile new democracy.

Conditions for ordinary South Africans in townships and in rural areas are unlikely to improve enough during the next few years to meet expectations. Poverty, competition for resources, and political intolerance remain factors that peace structures can help address effectively at the grassroots level. Ongoing training in conflict management skills, police-community relations, and local empowerment will be required.

To play such a role, however, the peace structures need to accept that the new circumstances require significant changes to the mandate under which they presently operate. The NPA requires important changes to make it relevant to postelection South Africa. The chapter dealing with socioeconomic reconstruction and development, for example, requires drastic revision. The new government is about to implement a sophisticated reconstruction program as its main priority. It will naturally want to claim credit for any improvement and will not look kindly on initiatives that operate independently of its own plan. Peace structures still have a role to play in that area, but the role should differ from the one presently defined in the accord. It will have to be a facilitating role that is complementary to the national reconstruction effort.

The parts of the accord dealing with the codes of conduct for security forces must also be amended. These are matters that the new government will incorporate into legislation and for which it will rightfully assume responsibility. The NPA also needs to become far more inclusive than it is at present. Different segments of civil society, not only political parties, ought to play key roles at all levels. Restructuring is required. A critical look needs to be taken at the role of the NPA, which has been inoperative for almost eighteen months. It should perhaps be merged with the NPS and trimmed to make it manageable. Most important, the main focus in the future ought to be on LPCs and the work they do at the grassroots level.

What is therefore required is a new round of inclusive negotiations to review and adapt the existing NPA. The peace structures should remain independent of government, with ownership vested in the communities they serve. Government funding will remain necessary, although more contributions from other sources should be obtained.

Peacemaking and peace building in South Africa will always have to remain a dynamic process. Continuous adaptations will therefore be necessary. The experiences gained and the goodwill earned are too valuable to dissipate. More effort ought to go into recording experiences. More research should be undertaken. The establishment of a South African Peace Institute would facilitate such work and would enable international experts and scholars to share in the South African experience and to contribute to the pool of knowledge. Other conflict-ridden societies could benefit from such an exchange of knowledge.

The struggle for reconciliation and development in South Africa is about to enter a new phase under the guidance of a government of national unity. Under the leadership of President Nelson Mandela and Deputy Presidents Thabo Mbeki and F. W. de Klerk, assisted by a population that has often surprised itself in situations of adversity, that struggle has every prospect of achieving its objectives. If the peace structures can claim even a tiny portion of the credit for successes along the way, then the dedication and tireless effort of thousands of peace workers throughout the country will have been worthwhile. They are, after all, the ones who made the peace structures work.

NOTES

1. Heribert Adam and Kogila Moodley, *The Negotiated Revolution* (Johannesburg: Jonathan Ball Press, 1993).

2. These negotiations resulted in agreements that were embodied in the Groote Schuur Minute of May 1990 and the Pretoria Minute of August 1990. The talks centered on mutual security issues, including the armed struggle, safe return of exiles, and the prospects for constitutional negotiations.

3. South African Institute of Race Relations, *Race Relations Survey 1991/92* (Johannesburg, 1992), p. 485.

4. From September 1, 1984, to September 30, 1993, a total of 17,636 persons were killed as a result of political violence (South African Institute of Race Relations, Johannesburg).

5. Anthony S. Mathews, *Freedom, State Security and the Rule of Law: Dilemmas of the Apartheid Society* (Cape Town: Juta, 1986).

6. Mathews, *Freedom, State Security*, p. 284.

7. South African Institute of Race Relations, *Race Relations Survey 1992/93* (Johannesburg, 1993), p. 255.

8. Mathews, *Freedom, State Security*, p. 284.

9. Development Bank of Southern Africa as cited on p. 9 in *South Africa 1993*, a pocket handbook issued by the South Africa Foundation, Johannesburg. "Indians" are descendants of Indian traders and indentured Indian laborers who arrived to work on the sugar cane plantations on the east coast (Natal) in the late 1880s. "Coloreds" are South Africans of mixed-race descent, based mainly in Cape Province.

10. South African Institute of Race Relations, Johannesburg.

11. Anthony Minnaar, Trevor Keith, and Catherine Payze, *SDUs or* Comtsotsis: *Criminal Gangs and Political Violence* (Pretoria: Centre for Conflict Analysis, Human Sciences Research Council, 1993).

12. Graeme Simpson, Steve Mokwena, and Laurel Segal, *Political Violence in 1990: The Year in Perspective* (Johannesburg: Project for the Study of Violence, Psychology Department, University of the Witwatersrand, 1991), p. 10.

13. André Du Toit, *Understanding South African Political Violence: A New Problematic?,* Occasional Research Paper (Geneva: UN Research Institute for Social Research, 1993), p. 4.

14. Maxwell Taylor, *The Fanatics: A Behavioural Approach to Political Violence* (London: Brassey's, 1991), p. 7.

15. Du Toit, *Understanding South African Political Violence*, p. 7.

16. South African Institute of Race Relations, *Fast Facts,* no. 6 (Johannesburg, 1993), p. 7.

17. Adam and Moodley, *The Negotiated Revolution*, p. 121. On p. 229 the authors provide a useful list of some of the more noteworthy academic works on political violence in South Africa.

18. Research carried out in the Pretoria-Witwatersrand-Vereeniging area over the 1970–84 period shows that the mere presence of security forces at events increased the subsequent rate of collective action by 39 percent, compared with events where they were absent. Antoinette Louw, "Political Conflict in Natal, 1989–1992," *Indicator South Africa* (Durban: Centre for Social and Development Studies, University of Natal), vol. 9, no. 3, 1992, p. 57.

19. Graham Howe, "The Trojan Horse: Natal's Civil War, 1987–1993," *Indicator South Africa*, vol. 10, no. 2, 1993, p. 35.

20. Anthony Minnaar, "Violent Natal," unpublished paper (Pretoria: Centre for Conflict Analysis, Human Sciences Research Council, 1993).

21. In the midst of the Seven Days' War a group of Natal members of Parliament, including the author, sought and had a meeting with President de Klerk to discuss the crisis. He undertook to send more security forces to the area but declined to take the initiative to call a meeting with Mandela and Buthelezi to address the political violence that was occurring.

22. *Cape Times*, December 10, 1990.

23. *Cape Times,* December 11, 1990.

24. At its congress on July 14, 1990, Inkatha shed its mantle as a Zulu cultural organization, renamed itself the Inkatha Freedom Party, and adopted a new constitution to convert itself into a conventional political party that would be open to all.

25. *Cape Times*, January 30, 1991.

26. *Cape Times*, February 1, 1991.

27. Human Rights Commission South Africa, *Special Report on Two Years of Destabilisation, July 1990 to June 1992*, SR-12 (Johannesburg, 1992).

28. *Business Day*, March 27, 1991.

29. South African Institute of Race Relations, *Race Relations Survey 1991/92*, p. 96.

30. *Johannesburg Sunday Times*, March 31, 1991.

31. *Johannesburg Sunday Times*, March 31, 1991.

32. The joint chairmen of CBM were Mike Sander (AECI) and Murray Hofmeyer (Argus). Others who constituted its twenty-four-member National Consultative Group included Neil Chapman (Southern Life), Simon Brand (Development Bank), Leon Cohen (PG Bisons), Peter Searle (Volkswagen),

Justin Schaffer (Property Group), Naas Steenkamp (Gencor), and Mike Spicer (Anglo American).

33. *Business Day*, April 17, 1991.

34. *Business Day*, April 18, 1991.

35. *Citizen*, April 19, 1991.

36. *Citizen*, April 19, 1991.

37. *Cape Times*, April 30, 1991.

38. *Business Day*, May 7, 1991.

39. *Die Burger*, May 4, 1991.

40. *Business Day*, May 10, 1991.

41. *Business Day*, May 16, 1991.

42. Colin Coleman, interview by author, Johannesburg, July 12, 1993.

43. Coleman, interview.

44. John Hall, interview by author, Johannesburg, July 12, 1993.

45. Hall, interview.

46. *Business Day*, May 20, 1991.

47. *Business Day*, May 20, 1991.

48. Others who had attended were Beyers Naude, Brigalia Bam, Murray Hofmeyer, Neil Chapman, Leon Cohen, John Hall, Debra Marsden, Theuns Eloff, Jay Naidoo, Raymond Parsons, and Andre Lamprecht.

49. Coleman, interview.

50. Coleman, interview.

51. South African Institute of Race Relations, *Race Relations Survey 1991/92*, p. 99.

52. Hall, interview.

53. Mangosuthu Buthelezi, "Action for Peace in South Africa: Some Observations and Some Specific Proposals," speech, May 24, 1991 (supplied by the IFP office in Johannesburg). The suggestion of a countrywide network of peace committees was eventually incorporated into the NPA.

54. *Pretoria News*, May 25, 1991.

55. *Pretoria News*, May 25, 1991.

56. Coleman, interview.

57. *Business Day*, May 25, 1991.

58. *Johannesburg Sunday Times*, May 26, 1991.

59. Human Rights Commission South Africa, *Special Report*.

60. Louw Alberts, interview by author, Pretoria, August 11, 1993.

61. Members of the facilitating committee were Louw Alberts (appointed at President de Klerk's peace summit), Frank Chikane (general secretary of the SACC), Sean Cleary (consultant, IFP confidant), Theuns Eloff (CBM), Bobby Godsell (Chamber of Mines representative), John Hall (president of SACOB),

Johan Heyns (former moderator, Dutch Reformed Church), Ray McCauley (head of Rhema Church), Sam Motsuenyane (president of National African Chambers of Commerce), Desmond Tutu (archbishop of Cape Town), Gerrie Lubbe (head of Interfaith), Jabu Mabuza (representative from FABCOS, a federation of African businesses), and Khoza Mgojo (president of the SACC).

62. Alberts, interview.

63. Alberts, interview.

64. Coleman, interview.

65. *Star*, June 13, 1991.

66. *Star*, June 22, 1991.

67. *Business Day*, June 24, 1991.

68. Thabo Mbeki (ANC), Roelf Meyer (National Party), and Frank Mdlalose (IFP).

69. Minutes of the meeting, CBM, Johannesburg.

70. The Conservative Party, the Afrikaner Weerstandsbeweging, and the Herstigte Nasionale Party.

71. *First Report of the Commonwealth Observer Mission to South Africa*, chap. 4, p. 44.

72. Coleman, interview.

73. Coleman, interview.

74. Disagreements focused mainly on the role of "private armies"—Umkhonto we Sizwe (the military wing of the ANC) and the KwaZulu Police, which the self-governing territory of KwaZulu deployed within its territory and which many regarded as the private army of the IFP. The future of some of the controversial units of the South African Defence Forces (e.g., Battalion 32) was also in dispute.

75. Although the NPS started to operate in November 1991, it was only on November 4, 1992, that it became a statutory body under recently passed legislation—the·Internal Peace Institutions Act, no. 135 of 1992.

76. Coleman, interview.

77. The National Party, the ANC alliance, and the IFP were, for example, represented by, among others, Roelf Meyer, Thabo Mbeki, and Frank Mdlalose, respectively.

78. Jayendra Naidoo (ANC alliance), Gert Myburgh MP (National Party), Suzanne Vos (IFP), Peter Gastrow MP (Democratic Party), Craven Collis (Labour Party), Antonie Gildenhuys (Association of Law Societies), and Deon Rudman (Department of Justice).

79. The eleven regions (and their main centers) were Far Northern Transvaal (Pietersburg), Eastern Transvaal (Middelburg), Witwatersrand-Vaal (Johannesburg), Northern Transvaal (Pretoria), Western Transvaal (Klerksdorp), Natal-KwaZulu (Durban), Border-Ciskei (East London), Eastern Cape (Port Elizabeth), Western Cape (Cape Town), Northern Cape (Kimberley), and Orange Free State (Bloemfontein).

80. Witwatersrand, the name of a range of hills in the Johannesburg area, refers to the greater metropolitan area of Johannesburg, while Vaal is the name of a river about an hour's drive south of Johannesburg.

81. At a meeting of the NPS and chairpersons of the regional committees it was decided that the name "dispute resolution committee" was too restrictive, and a change of names to "regional peace committee" and "local peace committee" was approved.

82. Official 1993 report of the NPS tabled in Parliament.

83. *Citizen*, June 24, 1993.

84. Chris de Kock, Cosmas Mareka, Nic Rhoodie, and Charl Schutte, *The Prospects for a Free, Democratic Election: Inhibiting and Facilitating Factors in Voting Intention* (Pretoria: Sociopolitical Monitoring and Analysis, Human Sciences Research Council, 1993).

85. *Middelburg Observer*, November 12, 1993.

86. *Sowetan*, November 8, 1993.

87. Hall, interview.

88. On June 17, 1992, an attack by hostel dwellers on the shack settlement of Boipatong in the southern Transvaal resulted in the deaths of forty-eight persons, mostly women and children. In protest against these deaths and the alleged role of the government in political violence, the ANC and its allies withdrew from the multiparty constitutional negotiations at CODESA on June 23, 1992, causing a collapse of the negotiating process. Certain demands were made to the government, and an unprecedented mass action campaign was announced. Mass protests were held, and tension in the country mounted, culminating in the ANC-organized march on the Ciskei capital, Bisho, which resulted in the deaths of twenty-nine persons, shot by Ciskei soldiers. The impasse in the negotiations lasted until September 26, 1992, when a "record of understanding" was signed between the ANC and the government. Buthelezi's response to this bilateral agreement was to announce the IFP's withdrawal from negotiations on September 27, 1992.

89. A recently passed law providing for optional mechanisms that would enable white-controlled local authorities and neighboring black townships to move toward a joint administration. The key role of the government-appointed provincial administrator in this process, as well as some other aspects of the law, has caused some controversy.

90. *The Report of the Commonwealth Observer Mission to South Africa to the Commonwealth Secretariat, February 1993–May 1993* (Johannesburg, 1993), p. 25.

91. Current programs of International Alert include seeking answers to international conflicts within the former Soviet Union and a focus on the rising tide of racism in Europe. International Alert has worked to resolve conflicts in Uganda, Guatemala, Kenya, Sri Lanka, the Philippines, and Tibet.

92. Participants in the evaluation mission were Neelan Tiruchelvam (Sri Lanka), Sue Williams (Northern Ireland), Eduardo Marino (Colombia), Edmundo

García (the Philippines), Chanthou Boua (Cambodia), Louise Nieuwmeijer (South Africa), Ampie Muller (South Africa), Saths Moodley (South Africa), and Vuyiswa Nxasana (South Africa).

93. International Alert, *Mission to Evaluate the National Peace Accord and Its Peace Structures Report* (London, 1993).

94. International Alert, *Mission*, chap. 3, "Analysis and Evaluation," p. 7.

95. *Citizen,* June 23, 1992.

96. South African Institute of Race Relations, *63rd Annual Report, 1/4/92 until 31/3/93* (Johannesburg, 1993).

97. *Report of the Commonwealth Observer Mission*, p. 26.

98. Among the victims were 16 train and taxi commuters, 47 women, 22 children, and 14 members of the security forces (Human Rights Commission, Johannesburg).

99. *Star*, September 15, 1992.

100. International Alert, *Mission*, p. 8.

101. Laurie Nathan, "An Imperfect Bridge: Crossing to Democracy on the Peace Accord," *Track Two* (Cape Town: Centre for Intergroup Studies), vol. 2, no. 2, 1993, p. 1.

102. The IFP has claimed that 300 of its officeholders have been killed since the NPA was signed in September 1991 (*Weekly Mail*, October 1–7, 1993).

103. Anthony Minnaar, Trevar Keith, and Sam Pretorius, *An Analysis of Massacres in South Africa, 1990–1992* (Pretoria: Centre for Conflict Analysis, Human Sciences Research Council, 1993).

104. Minnaar, "Violent Natal."

105. Mark Shaw, "War and Peace: Resolving Local Conflict," *Indicator South Africa*, vol. 10, no. 3, 1993, p. 63.

106. Angela King, chief of mission of the UN Observer Mission, in a speech delivered on May 11, 1993, in East London: "But while the absence of political tolerance continues to undermine the peace process, probably the single most important and intractable source of violence is to be found in the appalling socio-economic conditions under which the majority of people live."

107. South African Institute of Race Relations, *Race Relations Survey 1992/93*, p. 206.

108. Mike Morris and Doug Hindson, "South Africa: Political Violence, Reform and Reconstruction," *Review of African Political Economy*, no. 53, pp. 43–59.

109. NPS meeting held on June 3–4, 1993, in Kurgersdorp.

110. Manuscript copy, NPS office, Pretoria.

111. International Alert, *Mission*, p. 8.

112. The ANC received 62.7 percent of the national vote and thus 252 of the 400 parliamentary seats, the National Party 20.4 percent (82 seats), the IFP 10.5 percent (43 seats), the Freedom Front 2.2 percent (9 seats), the Democratic

Party 1.7 percent (7 seats), the PAC 1.2 percent (5 seats), and the African Christian Democratic Party 0.5 percent (2 seats).

113. *Citizen*, December 2, 1993.

114. *Citizen*, May 17, 1994.

115. Monthly summary reports on repression, Human Rights Commission, Johannesburg.

116. Jayendra Naidoo, "The Role of and Options Available to the Training Committee of the National Peace Secretariat," unpublished discussion paper (Johannesburg: National Peace Secretariat, 1994).

APPENDIX
Text of the
National
Peace Accord

Reprinted below is the complete text of the National Peace Accord, as presented at the National Peace Convention on September 14, 1991.

NATIONAL PEACE ACCORD

To signify our common purpose to bring an end to political violence in our country and to set out the codes of conduct, procedures and mechanisms to achieve this goal

WE, participants in the political process in South Africa, representing the political parties and organisations and governments indicated beneath our signatures, condemn the scourge of political violence which has afflicted our country and all such practices as have contributed to such violence in the past, and commit ourselves and the parties, organisations and governments we represent to this National Peace Accord.

The current prevalence of political violence in the country has already caused untold hardship, disruption and loss of life and property in our country. It now jeopardizes the very process of peaceful political transformation and threatens to leave a legacy of insurmountable division and deep bitterness in our country. Many, probably millions, of citizens live in continuous fear as a result of the climate of violence. This dehumanising factor must be eliminated from our society.

In order to achieve some measure of stability and to consolidate the peace process, a priority shall be the introduction of reconstruction actions aimed at addressing the worst effects of political violence at a local level. This would achieve a measure of stability based on common effort thereby facilitating a base for broader socio-economic development.

Reconstruction and developmental actions of the communities as referred to above, shall be conducted within the wider context of socio-economic development.

In order to effectively eradicate intimidation and violence, mechanisms need to be created which shall on the one hand deal with the investigation of incidents and the causes of violence and intimidation and on the other hand actively combat the occurrence of violence and intimidation.

The police force, which by definition shall include the police forces of all self-governing territories, has a central role to play in terminating the violence and in preventing the future perpetration of such violence. However, the perception of the past role of the police has engendered suspicion and distrust between the police and many of the affected communities. In recognition of the need to promote more effective policing, a commitment to sound policing practices and a co-operative relationship between the police and the communities are necessary.

This Accord is intended to promote peace and prosperity in violence-stricken communities. The right of all people to live in peace and harmony will be promoted by the implementation of this Accord.

The Accord is of such a nature that every peace-loving person can support it. The Accord reflects the values of all key players in the arena of negotiation and reconciliation.

The implementation and monitoring of the Peace Accord represents a crucial phase in the process to restore peace and prosperity to all the people of South Africa.

Noting that the majority of South Africans are God-fearing citizens, we ask for His blessing, care and protection upon our Nation to fulfil the trust placed upon us to ensure freedom and security for all.

Bearing in mind the values which we hold, be these religious or humanitarian, we pledge ourselves with integrity of purpose to make this land a prosperous one where we can all live, work and play together in peace and harmony.

The signatories have agreed upon:

- a Code of Conduct for political parties and organisations to be followed by all the political parties and organisations that are signatories to this Accord;
- a Code of Conduct to be adhered to by every police official to the best of his or her ability, as well as a detailed agreement on the security forces;
- the guidelines for the reconstruction and development of the communities;
- the establishment of mechanisms to implement the provisions of this Accord.

The signatories acknowledge that the provisions of this Peace Accord are subject to existing laws, rules and procedures and budgetary constraints. New structures should not be created where appropriate existing structures can be used.

This Accord will not be construed so as to detract from the validity of bilateral agreements between any of the signatories.

> *WE, the signatories, accordingly solemnly bind ourselves to this accord and shall ensure as far as humanly possible that all our members and supporters will comply with the provisions of this accord and will respect its underlying rights and values and we, the government signatories, undertake to pursue the objectives of this accord and seek to give effect to its provisions by way of the legislative, executive and budgeting procedures to which we have access.*

Chapter 1

Principles

1.1   The establishment of a multi-party democracy in South Africa is our common goal. Democracy is impossible in a climate of violence, intimidation and fear. In order to ensure democratic political activity all political participants must recognise and uphold certain fundamental rights described below and the corresponding responsibilities underlying those rights.

1.2   These fundamental rights include the right of every individual to:

- freedom of conscience and belief;

- freedom of speech and expression;

- freedom of association with others;

- peaceful assembly;

- freedom of movement;

- participate freely in peaceful political activity.

1.3   The fundamental rights and responsibilities derive from established democratic principles namely:

- democratic sovereignty derives from the people, whose right it is to elect their government and hold it accountable at the polls for its conduct of their affairs;

- the citizens must therefore be informed and aware that political parties and the media must be free to impart information and opinion;

- there should be an active civil society with different interest groups freely participating therein;

- political parties and organisations, as well as political leaders and other citizens, have an obligation to refrain from incitement to violence and hatred.

1.4   The process of reconstruction and socio-economic development aimed at addressing the causes of violent conflict, must be conducted in a non-partisan manner, that is, without being controlled by any political organisation or being to the advantage of any political group at the expense of another.

1.5   Reconstruction and developmental projects must actively involve the affected communities. Through a process of inclusive negotiations involving recipients, experts and donors, the community must be able to conceive, implement and take responsibility for projects in a co-ordinated way as close to the grassroots as possible. In addition, reconstruction and development must facilitate the development of the economic and human resources of the communities concerned.

1.6   The initiatives referred to in 1.4 and 1.5 above, should in no way abrogate the right and duty of governments to continue their normal developmental activity, except that in doing so they should be sensitive to the spirit and contents of any agreement that may be reached in terms of 1.5 above.

1.7   The parties to this process commit themselves to facilitating the rapid removal of political, legislative and administrative obstacles to development and economic growth.

1.8   The implementation of a system to combat violence and intimidation will only succeed if the parties involved have a sincere commitment to reach this objective. Only then will all the people of South Africa be able to fulfil their potential and create a better future.

1.9   It is clear that violence and intimidation declines when it is inves-
        tigated and when the background and reasons for it is exposed
        and given media attention. There is, therefore, need for an effec-
        tive instrument to do just that. It is agreed that the Commission
        established by the Prevention of Public Violence and Intimida-
        tion Act, 1991, be used as an instrument to investigate and
        expose the background and reasons for violence, thereby reduc-
        ing the incidence of violence and intimidation.

1.10   Since insufficient instruments exist to actively prevent violence
        and intimidation at regional and local levels, it is agreed that
        committees be appointed at regional and local levels to assist in
        this regard. Peace bodies are therefore to be established at both
        regional and local levels to be styled "Regional Dispute Resolution
        Committees" (RDRC) and "Local Dispute Resolution Commit-
        tees" (LDRC) respectively. These bodies will be guided and co-
        ordinated at a national level by a National Peace Secretariat. At the
        local level the bodies will be assisted by Justices of the Peace.

1.11   The Preparatory Committee has played a crucial role in the process
        of bringing the major actors together to negotiate a Peace Accord.
        There is still much to be done to implement the Accord and estab-
        lish the institutions of peace. To assist in this regard, a National
        Peace Committee shall be established.

1.12   There should be simple and expeditious procedures for the res-
        olution of disputes regarding transgressions of the Code for
        Political Parties and Organisations by political parties and organ-
        isations who are signatories to the National Peace Accord. These
        disputes should wherever possible, be settled at grassroots level,
        through participation of the parties themselves; and by using
        the proven methods of mediation, arbitration and adjudication.

1.13   An effective and credible criminal judicial system requires the
        swift and just dispensation of justice. This in turn will promote
        the restoration of peace and prosperity to communities, freeing
        them of the ravages of violence and intimidation. Special attention
        should be given to unrest related cases by setting up Special
        Criminal Courts specifically for this purpose.

Chapter 2

Code of Conduct for Political Parties and Organisations

The signatories to this Accord agree to the following Code of Conduct:

2.1   We recognise the essential role played by political parties and organisations as mediators in a democratic political process, permitting the expression, aggregation and reconciliation of different views and interests, and facilitating the translation of the outcome of this process into law and public policy, and respect the activities of political parties and organisations in organising their respective structures, canvassing for support, arranging and conducting public meetings, and encouraging voting.

2.2   All political parties and organisations shall actively contribute to the creation of a climate of democratic tolerance by:

- publicly and repeatedly condemning political violence and encouraging among their followers an understanding of the importance of democratic pluralism and a culture of political tolerance; and

- acting positively, also *vis-a-vis* all public authorities including local and traditional authorities, to support the right of all political parties and organisations to have reasonable freedom of access to their members, supporters and other persons in rural and urban areas, whether they be housed on public or private property.

2.3   No political party or organisation or any official or representative of any such party, shall:

- kill, injure, apply violence to, intimidate or threaten any other person in connection with that person's political beliefs, words, writings or actions;

- remove, disfigure, destroy, plagiarise or otherwise misrepresent any symbol or other material of any other political party or organisation;

- interfere with, obstruct or threaten any other person or group travelling to or from or intending to attend, any gathering for political purposes;

- seek to compel, by force or threat of force, any person to join any party or organisation, attend any meeting, make any contribution, resign from any post or office, boycott any occasion or commercial activity or withhold his or her labour or fail to perform a lawful obligation; or

- obstruct or interfere with any official or representative of any other political party or organisation's message to contact or address any group of people.

2.4   All political parties and organisations shall respect and give effect to the obligation to refrain from incitement to violence or hatred. In pursuit hereof no language calculated or likely to incite violence or hatred, including that directed against any political party or personality, nor any wilfully false allegation, shall be used at any political meeting, nor shall pamphlets, posters or other written material containing such language be prepared or circulated, either in the name of any party, or anonymously.

2.5   All political parties and organisations shall:

- ensure that the appropriate authorities are properly informed of the date, place, duration and, where applicable, routing of each public meeting, rally, march or other event organised by the party or organisation;

- take into account local sentiment and foreseeable consequences, as well as any other meetings already arranged on the same date in close proximity to the planned event, provided that this shall not detract from the right of any political party or organisation freely to propagate its political views; and

- immediately and at all times, establish and keep current effective lines of communication between one another at national, regional and local levels, by ensuring a reciprocal exchange of the correct names, addresses and contact numbers of key leaders at each level, and by appointing liaison personnel in each location to deal with any problems which may arise.

2.6   All political parties and organisations shall provide full assistance and co-operation to the police in the investigation of violence and the apprehension of individuals involved. The signatories to this Accord specifically undertake not to protect or harbour their members and supporters to prevent them from being subjected to the processes of justice.

Chapter 3

Security Forces: General Provisions

3.1   General Principles

3.1.1   The police shall endeavour to protect the people of South Africa from all criminal acts and shall do so in a rigorously non-partisan fashion, regardless of the political belief and affiliation, race, religion, gender or ethnic origin of the perpetrators or victims of such acts.

3.1.2   The police shall endeavour to prevent crimes and shall attempt to arrest and investigate all those reasonably suspected of committing crimes and shall take the necessary steps to facilitate the judicial process.

3.1.3   The police shall be guided by a belief that they are accountable to society in rendering their policing services and shall therefore conduct themselves so as to secure and retain the respect and approval of the public. Through such accountability and friendly, effective and prompt service, the police shall endeavour to obtain the co-operation of the public whose partnership in the task of crime control and prevention is essential.

3.1.4   The police, as law enforcement officers, shall expect a higher standard of conduct from its members in the execution of their duties than they expect from others and in pursuance hereof, supports prompt and efficient investigation and prosecution of its own members alleged to have acted unlawfully and shall commit itself to continue the proper training and retraining of its members in line with the objectives of professional policing and the principles set out in Chapters 3 and 4 of this Accord. The police in particular shall emphasise that there is no place in the police force for policing practices based on personal or racial prejudice, corruption, excessive force or any unlawful actions.

3.1.5   The police shall exercise restraint in the pursuance of their duties and shall use the minimum force that is appropriate in the circumstances.

3.1.6   Parties, organisations and individuals acknowledge that they too have a contribution to make in the process of sustaining, developing and encouraging a police force of which all South Africans can be proud. This involves a respect for the professionalism of the police force, and assisting the police in the performance of their legitimate duties.

3.2   The police shall observe the following more detailed set of requirements:

3.2.1   The police shall endeavour to protect the people of South Africa from all criminal acts and acts of political violence, and shall do so in a rigorously non-partisan fashion, regardless of the political belief and affiliation, religion, gender, race, or ethnic origin of the perpetrators or victims of such acts.

3.2.1.1 The police must always respond promptly to calls for assistance and intervention.

3.2.1.2 Where prior notification is given of possible violence, the police must take all reasonable steps to prevent such an outbreak of violence.

3.2.1.3 The police shall endeavour to disarm those persons illegally bearing dangerous weapons in any gathering or procession.

3.2.2   The police shall endeavour to prevent crimes and shall attempt to arrest and investigate all those reasonably suspected of committing crimes and shall take the necessary steps to facilitate the judicial process.

3.2.2.1 Where violent clashes occur the police shall attempt to arrest all those reasonably suspected of participating in any unlawful act. If the police are unable for any reason to arrest all suspects, efforts must be made to photograph, video or otherwise identify the suspects.

3.2.2.2 After a suspect has been arrested, the police shall conduct a full, proper and expeditious investigation into the complaint, shall endeavour to submit the necessary evidence to the Attorney-General as soon as possible and shall give all the necessary co-operation in this regard.

3.2.2.3 In addition to rights arrested persons have in terms of the law, suspects arrested solely for crimes related to political violence should be informed of their rights and given the opportunity to telephone their family or a lawyer. Judges' Rules shall consistently be applied by all police officials.

3.2.2.4 All criminal complaints shall be accepted at a charge office. After the complaint is accepted, the complainant shall be given a form containing the complaint number and the nature of the charge. The name and the telephone number of the investigating officer shall be made available or dispatched within seven days to the complainant.

3.2.2.5 The complainant shall, upon request, be entitled to any relevant information from the investigating officer on the progress and outcome of the investigation.

3.2.2.6 In order to investigate all crimes relating to "political violence", which includes public violence as defined in the Prevention of Public Violence and Intimidation Act, 1991, the police shall establish a special police investigation unit on the following basis:

    (i) A police investigation unit shall be established under the command of a police general (or senior police officer in the case of self-governing territories).

    (ii) This police general shall monitor, co-ordinate and supervise investigations into crimes of political violence.

    (iii) A senior police officer shall be appointed in the region of each special criminal court and shall carry out his duties and functions under the command of the said police general.

(iv)   It will be the responsibility of each such officer as assisted by such officials as are seconded to him or appointed on an *ad hoc* basis to assist him, to conduct or supervise investigations into crimes of political violence, in the region of that special criminal court.

(v)   When necessary each such officer shall liaise with the prosecutor of the special court in regard to the conduct of investigations into crimes of political violence.

(vi)   Each such officer may personally investigate such crimes and/or supervise investigations performed by ordinary units of the police.

(vii) The police general who commands the special investigation unit as well as each such officer shall, where possible, have sufficient personnel and resources at his disposal to enable him to effectively carry out his powers and functions.

(viii) Each such officer shall be responsible for compiling a monthly report on the progress of investigations and for referring it to the police general who commands the special investigation unit. The Standing Commission and/or the National Peace Committee may inquire on the progress of the investigations and the police general shall submit a report.

(ix)   In all cases where an affidavit containing evidence is submitted to the National Peace Committee or Regional Dispute Resolution Committee to the effect that the local police in any station and/or district have acted with bias towards a political party or organisation in that district, the investigation into any incident of alleged political violence shall, on basis of the affidavit, be conducted by the special investigation unit with jurisdiction in that region or under the supervision of an officer from such unit.

(x)   The National Peace Committee shall be informed of the appointment of the police general and the senior officers.

(xi)   The Commissioner of Police shall have regard to recommendations of the National Peace Committee.

3.2.3   The police shall be guided by a belief that they are accountable to society in rendering their policing services and shall therefore conduct themselves so as to secure and retain the respect and approval of the public.

Accountability in this paragraph and also referred to in clause 3.1.3 above, as well as in the Police Code of conduct, entails the following:

3.2.3.1 In order to facilitate better communication with the community, the police shall, in each locality where a Local Dispute Resolution Committee exists:

(i)   consult regularly with:

(a) the Local Dispute Resolution Committee, or in its absence, community leaders, including representatives of signatories to this Accord, and

(b) community leaders,

on the efficient functioning of the police in that community and shall regularly communicate with such committee, representatives or leaders on the issues raised by them with the police.

(ii)   establish a liaison officer of rank not lower than a warrant officer, in each police district, to which requests for urgent assistance may be directed. The police shall notify the LDRC of the identity of liaison officers.

3.2.3.2 In addition to the normal channels available within the Department of Law and Order, complaints against the police may also be referred to the Police Reporting Officer or, depending on the nature of such complaints, to the Standing Commission on Violence and Intimidation.

3.2.3.3 If the police feel that they are unfairly victimised or harassed by any person or body or organisation they will have the right to raise a complaint to the National Peace Committee or any other appropriate body.

3.2.4   The police shall expect a higher standard of conduct from themselves than they expect from others.

3.2.4.1 Complaints of alleged police misconduct which is of such a serious nature that it may detrimentally affect police/community relations should be referred to the Police Reporting Officer or the Commissioner of Police, for investigation by a unit of the police specifically established for this purpose, under the supervision of a designated general of the police. Where the complaint is directed to the Police Reporting Officer it should be referred by him to the Commissioner of Police for investigation by such a unit. The units will be available as far as possible in each police region.

3.2.4.2 The unit shall submit to the Police Reporting Officer, a report on the complaints submitted to it, as well as the progress and outcome of investigations into complaints. The Police Reporting Officer will have the authority to ensure that the investigation is a full and proper investigation and accordingly will be entitled to refer the report back to the unit. The Police Reporting Officer shall be appointed in the following manner:

   (i)   The Association of Law Societies and General Council of the Bar shall recommend to the Minister of Law and Order three candidates per region for the appointment of a Regional Police Reporting Officer. If the Minister is not prepared to make an appointment from the names so received, he may refer the recommendation back to the Association of Law Societies and the General Council of the Bar for additional three names from which he has to make an appointment.

   (ii)   Such Police Reporting Officer may be a former prosecutor, a former member of the attorney general's staff, a lawyer in private practice, a former magistrate, or a former policeman.

3.2.4.3 The Police Reporting Officer may recommend to the Commissioner of Police the suspension or transfer of the police official under investigation until the completion of the investigation.

3.2.4.4 The Police Reporting Officer shall, on the completion of the investigation, make a recommendation to the Commissioner of Police as to the disciplinary action that should be taken against the police involved in the misconduct. The complainant shall be notified of the recommendations and the outcome of this complaint. The Police Reporting Officer may, with the consent of the complainant, provide the National Peace Committee with the recommendations and outcome of the investigation.

3.2.4.5 All police officials in uniform should carry a legible external form of identification.

3.2.4.6 All official police vehicles shall have an identification number painted on the side, and all military vehicles acting in support of the police shall display an identification number on the side and no such number may be removed for as long as such military vehicles are used in support of the police, provided that this shall not apply to police vehicles which are required for official undercover work, not in breach of clause 3.5 related to clandestine or covert operations. It shall be an offence for a police or military vehicle to be driven on a public road without numberplates or without the numberplates allocated to such vehicle by the relevant registration authority.

3.2.5 The police shall exercise restraint in the pursuance of their duties and shall use the minimum force that is appropriate in the circumstances.

3.2.5.1 Clear guidelines shall be issued by the police for dealing with unlawful gatherings and the following aspects shall clearly be addressed in such guidelines.

    (i)   When a confrontation between a police unit and a gathering is reasonably foreseeable, a senior police official shall, where possible, be in command of that unit.

    (ii)   The police unit performing crowd control duties shall, where possible, be equipped with public address systems and someone who can address the crowd in a language the crowd will understand.

(iii)   Before ordering a gathering to disperse, an attempt must be made to ascertain the purpose of the gathering and to negotiate the immediate dispersal of the group.

(iv)   Where residents of a community or a hostel are clearly the subject of an attack, the police shall endeavour to disarm and disperse the aggressors.

(v)   A reasonable time must be given to the gathering to comply with the requests or instructions of the commanding officer.

(vi)   The commanding officer shall only authorise the use of injurious or forceful methods of crowd dispersal if he believes that the crowd constitutes a danger to the public safety or to the safety of any individual or to any valuable movable or immovable property and if he has reason to believe that less injurious methods will not succeed in dispersing the gathering. The least possible degree of force should be used in attaining the aim of policing. Unless circumstances prevent it, persuasion, advice and warnings should be used to secure co-operation, compliance with the law and the restoration of order.

(vii)   The police should focus on making less injurious equipment also available to police stations in order to minimize the risk of forceful actions.

3.3   Police Board

3.3.1   A Police Board shall be established whose composition shall comprise of both members of the public and representatives of the police in equal numbers. The chairperson is to be appointed by the Minister of Law and Order from one of the members representing the public.

3.3.2   The members of the public shall be appointed by the Minister of Law and Order to the Police Board from names put forward by unanimous decision by the National Peace Committee. The Minister of Law and Order shall have the discretion to appoint further members from parties who are not represented on the National Peace Committee.

3.3.3   The function of the Police Board shall be to consider and to make recommendations to the Minister of Law and Order in regard to the policy relating to the training and efficient functioning of the police, with a view to reconcile the interests of the community with that of the police.

3.3.4   The Police Board shall be empowered to do research and call for representations from the public regarding any investigation conducted by it.

3.3.5   The Police Board shall not have a role in regard to the day to day functioning of the police.

3.3.6   The recommendations of the Police Board in regard to the above matters shall be made public, insofar as it is essential in reconciling the interests of the community with that of the police.

3.4   Composition of the Police Force

3.4.1   The relationship between, and the status of, the South African Police and the Police Forces in the Self-governing Territories in the transitional phase can only be decided by the interested parties through negotiations.

3.4.2   Where the Police Force of any self-governing territory is alleged to be a party to the conflict, the Standing Commission shall investigate this and make appropriate recommendations.

3.5   Clandestine or Covert Operations

3.5.1   No public funds shall be used to promote the interests of any political party or political organisation and no political party or political organisation shall accept any public funds to promote its interests which shall have the effect of interfering negatively in the political process.

3.5.2   The government shall not allow any operation by the security forces with the intention to undermine, promote or influence any political party or political organisation at the expense of another by means of any acts, or by means of disinformation.

3.5.3   If any of the signatories to this Accord has reason to believe that any operation is being conducted in breach of this clause, it may lodge a complaint with the Police Reporting Officer or the Commission as the case may be.

3.5.4   In addition to any civil/criminal liability he/she may incur, any individual member of the police who is found to have breached this clause shall be dealt with in accordance with the Police Act, Regulations and Standing Orders.

3.5.5   In addition to any civil/criminal liability he/she may incur, any individual member of the defence force who is found to have breached this clause shall be dealt with in accordance with the defence statutes and codes and the Code of Conduct for the members of the defence force.

3.5.6   In order to monitor ongoing compliance with this provision the Commission, or a person authorised by it, shall upon receipt of any request by a party, or a complaint or on information received by it, be entitled by warrant to enter and inspect any place and interrogate any security force member, and seize any record or piece of evidence.

3.6.   Dangerous Weapons

3.6.1   The parties agree that the disastrous consequences of widespread violence and the urgent requirement of peace and stability on which to build the common future make it necessary to act decisively to eliminate violence or the threat of violence from a political sphere.

3.6.2   In pursuit of this understanding the parties agree that no weapons or fire-arms may be possessed, carried or displayed by members of the general public attending any political gathering, procession or meeting.

3.6.3   All political parties and organisations shall actively discourage and seek to prevent their members and supporters from possessing, carrying or displaying weapons or fire-arms when attending any political gathering, procession or meeting.

3.6.4   The Government undertakes to issue the necessary proclama-
        tions to implement the principles of paragraph 3.6.2 after con-
        sultation with the interested parties.

3.7   Self-Protection Units (previously called self-defence units)

3.7.1   The Law accords all individuals the right to protect themselves
        and their property, and to establish voluntary associations or self
        protection units in any neighbourhood to prevent crime and to
        prevent any invasion of the lawful rights of such communities.
        This shall include the right to bear licensed arms and to use
        them in legitimate and lawful self-defence.

3.7.2   The parties also agree that no party or political organisation shall
        establish such units on the basis of party or political affiliation,
        such units being considered private armies.

3.7.3   No private armies shall be allowed or formed.

3.7.4   The parties also recognise that a liaison structure should operate
        between any community based self protection unit and the police
        so as to facilitate education on citizens' rights, police responsive-
        ness and other aspects in respect of which there is a legitimate
        and common interest.

3.7.5   The police remains responsible for the maintenance of law and
        order and shall not be hindered in executing their task by any
        self protection unit.

3.7.6   All existing structures called self-defence units shall be trans-
        formed into self protection units which shall function in accor-
        dance with the principles contained in paragraph 3.7.

3.8   General

3.8.1   This Accord shall, where applicable, be issued as a directive by
        the Commissioner of Police and if necessary, the Police Act and
        regulations will be amended accordingly.

3.8.2   In view of the changing policing demands of a changing South
        Africa the police shall continue to take steps to retrain their
        members on the proper functions of the police as set out in the
        Code and in this agreement and in particular in methods of
        defusing conflict through discussion.

3.8.3 This Accord shall, where applicable, be honoured by and shall in terms of paragraph 3.8.1 be binding on the police.

3.8.4 This Accord shall, where applicable, be binding on the defence force in as much as it performs any ordinary policing function.

3.8.5 Where a government of a self-governing territory becomes a signatory to this Accord, the provisions of this Accord will, *mutatis mutandis,* be applicable to such a government as well as the police force of such a government.

3.8.6 A government of a self-governing territory which is a signatory to this Accord may opt to accept the jurisdiction of the Police Board or Police Reporting Officer established in respect of the South African Police Force.

3.9 Code of Conduct for Members of the Defence Force

A Code is in the process of being negotiated under the auspices of the National Peace Committee.

Chapter 4

Security Forces: Police Code of Conduct

MISSION OF THE SOUTH AFRICAN POLICE

"We undertake, impartially and with respect for the norms of the law and society, to protect the interests of the country and everyone therein against any criminal violation, through efficient service rendered in an accountable manner."

CODE OF CONDUCT OF THE SOUTH AFRICAN POLICE

All members of the South African Police shall commit themselves to abide by the Code of Conduct in the following terms:

As a member of the South African Police, I undertake to adhere to the following Code of Conduct to the best of my abilities:

As POLICE OFFICIAL I will observe the oath of loyalty which I made to the Republic of South Africa by performing the task that is required of me by law, with untiring zeal, single-mindedness and devotion to duty, realising that I accept the following principles:

- In order to preserve the fundamental and constitutional rights of each individual by the use of preventive measures, or alternatively, in the event of disruption, to restore social order by the use of reactive policing.

- The authority and powers accorded to the Police for the maintenance of social order, and the subsidiary objectives they adopt are dependent upon and subject to public approval, and the ability to secure and retain the respect of the public.

- The attainment and retention of public approval and respect include the co-operation of the public in the voluntary observance of the laws.

- Any offence or alleged offence by any member of the South African Police, of the common law or statutory law, including the Police Act and the regulations promulgated in accordance thereof, shall be thoroughly investigated and in the event of any violation thereof, appropriate measures shall be taken. Such an offence or alleged offence, depending on the nature thereof, may be referred to a Police Reporting Officer or the Commission established in terms of the Prevention of Violence and Intimidation Act, 1991, or to a commission that shall be specifically appointed for that purpose. All assistance and co-operation possible shall be rendered to a commission such as this, and the Police Reporting Officer, and where investigations are undertaken by the Police at the request of the commission or the Police Reporting Officer, a special investigation team shall be used for this purpose.

- The extent and quality of public co-operation proportionally diminishes the need for corrective measures.

  The favour and approval of the public shall be sought by:

    — enforcing the law firmly, sensitively and with constant and absolute impartiality;

- giving effective and friendly service to each individual, regardless of the political and religious belief, race, gender or ethnic origin;

- reacting as quickly as possible on requests for help or service;

- making personal sacrifices in order to save lives; and

- encouraging police-community relationships, and by promoting participation by the community.

• The least possible degree of force be used in attaining the aim of policing, and then only when persuasion, advice and warnings have falled to secure co-operation, compliance with the law and the restoration of order.

• Judges' Rules shall consistently be applied by all police officials.

• Police officials must adhere to the executive function of policing and refrain from taking it upon themselves to perform a judicial function.

• All police officials in uniform shall wear a clearly distinguishable mark of identification.

• The integrity of policing is reflected by the degree of personal moral responsibility and professional altruism evident in the behaviour and actions of every individual member of the police.

• The stability of society, and the vitality and continuity of democratic ideals are dependent upon policing that:

- is consistently aware of the sensitive balance between individual freedom and collective security;

- is consistently aware of the dangers inherent in illegal and informal coercive actions and methods; and

- will never give in to the temptation to sacrifice principles by resorting to reprehensible means to secure good ends.

• The professionalisation of policing depends primarily upon intensive selection, training, planning and research.

- The needs of the community shall be considered in the training programme of the Police, and the contribution made by communities in this regard, shall be taken into account.

- Every member should strive and apply him/herself to individual and institutional professionalism by self-improvement and study.

- Any offence by any member of the police, committed in the presence of a fellow member of the police, shall be dealt with by such a fellow member in accordance with the powers and duties conferred upon him or her by any act relating to such an offence. In addition such a fellow member shall forthwith notify his or her commander.

In order to maintain these principles, I undertake to:

- make my personal life an example worthy to be followed by all;

- develop my own personality and also create the opportunity for others to do likewise;

- treat my subordinates as well as my seniors in a decent manner;

- fulfil my duty faithfully despite danger, insult or threat;

- develop self-control, remain honest in thought and deed, both on and off duty;

- be an example in obeying the law of the land and the precepts of the Force;

- prevent personal feelings, prejudice, antagonism or friendships from influencing my judgement;

- receive no unlawful reward or compensation; and

- remain worthy of the trust of the public, by unselfish service, seek satisfaction in being ready to serve and to dedicate myself in the service to my God and my country.

"SERVAMUS ET SERVIMUS—WE PROTECT AND WE SERVE"

Chapter 5

Measures to Facilitate Socio-Economic
Reconstruction and Development

5.1   Reconstruction and development projects must actively involve
       the affected communities. Through a process of inclusive nego-
       tiations involving recipients, experts and donors, the community
       must be able to conceive, implement and take responsibility for
       projects in a co-ordinated way as close to the grassroots as pos-
       sible. In addition reconstruction and development must facilitate
       the development of the economic and human resources of the
       communities concerned.

5.2   Projects at a local level require the co-operation of all members
       of the community irrespective of their political affiliation. The
       people within local communities must see local organisations
       working together on the ground with common purpose. Parties
       with constituency support in an area must commit themselves
       to facilitating such an approach to development projects.

5.3   Reconstruction projects must work on the ground at local level.
       This requires a combined effort by all political organisations and
       affected parties to raise the required level of capital and human
       resources for development. Public and private funds will have to
       be mobilised for this purpose.

5.4   Sustainable development implies that all individuals must be
       assisted and encouraged to accept responsibility for their socio-
       economic well-being. Each actor must define and accept his/her
       role and there must be an acceptance of co-responsibility for
       and co-determination of socio-economic development.

5.5   This development initiative should in no way abrogate the right
       and duty of governments to continue their normal development
       activity, except that in doing so they should be sensitive to the
       spirit and contents of any agreement that may be reached.

5.6   The parties to this process commit themselves to facilitating the
       rapid removal of political, legislative and administrative obsta-
       cles to development and economic growth.

5.7   The National Peace Committee and the Regional Dispute Reso-
        lution Committees will establish permanent sub-committees on
        socio-economic reconstruction and development.

5.8   Both the national and regional sub-committees defined above
        could establish advisory and consulting groups to facilitate
        their work.

5.9   The functions of these sub-committees would be to:

5.9.1   assist the peace structures in regard to socio-economic recon-
        struction and development;

5.9.2   take initiatives to implement the principles outlined above and
        to deal with the issues set out hereunder;

5.9.3   the combined inputs of the sub-committees' participants would
        be to facilitate, co-ordinate and expedite reconstruction and devel-
        opment in terms of the principles outlined above.

5.10   The general guideline on issues to be dealt with is to move from
        immediate issues related to violence and the peace process towards
        pre-emption of violence and then towards integrating into the
        overall need for socio-economic development.

5.11   The sub-committees should identify areas at community level
        where they could begin to facilitate the co-ordination of the fol-
        lowing issues:

        • reconstruction of damaged property;

        • reintegration of displaced persons into the community;

        • expansion of infrastructure to assist in consolidating the
          peace process; and

        • community involvement in the maintenance and
          improvement of existing community facilities and the
          environment.

5.12   The sub-committees should facilitate crisis assistance that will
        link to socio-economic development in the following areas:

- dealing with the immediate effects of violence and the resultant social effects, displaced persons problem and homelessness; and

- where infrastructure is itself a spark to violence, e.g. water, electricity, transportation, schools, etc.

5.13   In addressing the above issues attention will have to be paid to:

- the equitable allocation of state resources, including state-funded development agencies (physical and financial) for both public and community-based initiatives;

- mobilisation of additional resources—both public and private;

- the cumbersome nature of governmental structures in the provision of resources and services;

- the position of the very poor and marginalised groups;

- land, its accessibility and use;

- basic housing;

- provision of basic services;

- education;

- health and welfare;

- job-creation and unemployment; and

- the availability of land for housing and basic services.

5.14   The sub-committees should identify potential flash points and co-ordinate socio-economic development that will defuse tension, e.g. squatter settlements: squatter settlement–township interfaces; hostels: hostel-township interfaces, provision and maintenance of basic services and rural resource constraints. The sub-committees should identify areas of socio-economic development that would prevent violence.

5.15   The sub-committee would attempt to ensure that overall socio-economic development is cognizant of the need to reinforce the peace process and defuse the potential for violence.

Chapter 6

Commision of Inquiry Regarding the Prevention of Public Violence and Intimidation ("the Commission")

6.1   It is acknowledged that the police is primarily responsible for the investigation of crime. The police is, as a result, also responsible for the investigation and bringing to book of all perpetrators of violence and intimidation.

6.2   *Post mortem* inquests play an important role in exposing and opening up circumstances relating to unrest and violence. Inquests with judges as presiding officers have taken place more frequently since the implementation of the Inquests Amendment Act, 1990 (Act 45 of 1990). The Inquests Amendment Act, 1991 (Act 8 of 1991), has furthermore streamlined the process and inquests can be disposed of more rapidly. Records of all inquest proceedings relating to public violence should be submitted to the Commission.

6.3   It is clear that violence and intimidation declines when it is investigated and when the background and reasons for it is exposed and given media attention. There is therefore need for an effective instrument to do just that. It is agreed that the Commission established by the Prevention of Public Violence and Intimidation Act, 1991, be used as an instrument to investigate and expose the background and reasons for violence, thereby reducing the incidence of violence and intimidation. However, in order to improve the efficacy of the Act in preventing violence it may be necessary to amend the Act, to accommodate the provisions of this Chapter. Where amendments are necessary, the National Peace Committee shall send its proposals to the Minister of Justice as soon as possible.

6.4   In terms of the Prevention of Public Violence and Intimidation Act, 1991, the Commission shall function as follows:

6.5   The Commission shall function on a permanent basis.

6.6   The Commission's objectives shall be to:

6.6.1   inquire into the phenomenon of public violence and intimida-
         tion in the Republic, the nature and causes thereof and what
         persons are involved therein;

6.6.2   inquire into any steps that should be taken in order to prevent
         public violence and intimidation;

6.6.3   make recommendations to the State President regarding:

6.6.3.1 the general policy which ought to be followed in respect of the
         prevention of public violence and intimidation;

6.6.3.2 steps to prevent public violence or intimidation;

6.6.3.3 any other steps it may deem necessary or expedient, including
         proposals for the passing of legislation, to prevent a repetition or
         continuation of any act of omission relating to public violence or
         intimidation;

6.6.3.4 the generation of income by the State to prevent public violence
         and intimidation as well as the compensating of persons who
         were prejudiced and suffered patrimonial loss thereby;

6.6.3.5 any other matter which may contribute to preventing public
         violence and intimidation.

6.7   It is agreed that the Commission shall be composed as follows:

6.7.1   A judge or retired judge of the Supreme Court or a senior advo-
         cate with at least 10 years experience in the enforcement of the
         law. This will ensure that the Commission has suitable, indepen-
         dent and objective leadership, fully versed in the law and fear-
         lessly given to grant all parties an equal opportunity to state
         their views and give their facts. This person will be the chairman.

6.7.2   A senior advocate or a senior attorney or a senior professor of
         law. The incumbent will assist the chairman of the Commission,
         providing balance from a legal point of view. Because of his sta-
         tus this person will not be susceptible to influence from other
         parties. This person will be the vice-chairman.

6.7.3   Three other duly qualified persons.

6.8   The National Peace Committee shall submit a short list of per-
         sons to be considered for appointment.

6.9   It is acknowledged that it is desirable that the Commission should be and be seen to be independent and non-partisan.

6.10   Members of the Commission are appointed for a period of three years.

6.11   The Commission will be assisted by a secretariat to provide administrative and logistical services.

6.12   The Commission's functions will include the following:

6.12.1 to investigate the causes of violence and intimidation;

6.12.2 to recommend measures capable of containing the cycle of violence;

6.12.3 to recommend measures in order to prevent further violence;

6.12.4 to initiate research programmes for the establishment of scientific empirical data on violence; and

6.12.5 to make recommendations concerning the funding of the process of peace.

6.13   Any individual will be able to approach the Commission with a request to investigate any particular matter relevant to combating violence and intimidation. If any such individual is held in detention, the relevant authorities will facilitate the transmission of such a request to the Commission. If a request is unfounded, trivial or designed for purposes other than the prevention of violence and intimidation, the Commission may in its discretion decline to act upon the request. The Commission does not only act upon receiving a request from an individual, but may of its own accord investigate matters.

6.14   The investigation by or at the behest of the Commission shall not affect any legal processes.

6.15   Where a matter has already been dealt with as a result of legal processes, the Commission shall not re-investigate the matter but may take cognizance of the evidence presented during such processes and the findings emanating from such proceedings.

6.16   The Commission shall be empowered to enlist the help of other institutions in its investigations. Investigations by the Police

Reporting Officer referred to in this Accord shall not be affected by the Commission.

6.17   Members of the Commission and its secretariat (insofar as they may not be employed by the State) shall be remunerated by the State. The State shall provide funds for the operation of the Commission.

6.18   The Commission shall be empowered in order to conduct an investigation and insofar as it may be relevant to:

6.18.1 require any person to give evidence on the matter being investigated;

6.18.2 require any person to put any document or other evidentiary material at the disposal of the Commission;

6.18.3 order that the identity of any person mentioned in 6.18.1 and 6.18.2 shall not be revealed if that person's life or property or his family may be endangered because of his assistance to the Commission;

6.18.4 order that the relevant authority provide appropriate protection to a person mentioned in 6.18.1 and 6.18.2 if his life is endangered because of his assistance to the Commission; and

6.18.5 order that the contents of any document or other evidentiary material shall not be revealed or published if circumstances so demand.

6.19   The proceedings of the Commission shall take place in public, unless the Commission decides that circumstances demand otherwise. This is designed to ensure that the safety of witnesses can be guaranteed.

6.20   The Commission shall determine if legal representation is desirable in any particular given case.

6.21   After completion of an investigation the Commission shall compile a report on its findings and recommendations. This report will be handed to the State President who may make known for public information the facts in question and the findings of the Commission which he deems necessary in the public interest. Without derogating from the State President's discretion, the

State President is requested to make such reports available to *inter alia* the National Peace Committee.

6.22   Measures shall be enacted to provide for the expenses and mechanisms of the Commission.

6.23   In order to ensure that steps are taken against perpetrators of violence and intimidation, the Commission may refer any evidence constituting an offence to the relevant Attorney-General and to the Special Criminal Courts.

6.24   Anyone hampering or influencing the Commission or any of its members in the execution of their duties shall be guilty of an offence. This will ensure that the status of the Commission is established and that it does not fall prey to pressures.

6.25   The above-mentioned is reflected in the Prevention of Public Violence and Intimidation Act, 1991.

6.26   Fully aware of the fact that the composition of the proposed body will determine its relevancy and legitimacy, the Minister of Justice indicated during the Second Reading Debate of the Act that no appointments would be made without consultation and negotiation with the relevant role players. Consensus will be the key word. It is agreed that for this system to be effective, it needs to be credible.

6.27   In terms of section 4 of the Act, committees may be established to assist the Commission in the exercise of its functions. The relevant players will therefore also be able to be represented on these committees by their own members and experts. These committees will enjoy the same far-reaching powers as the Commission itself. Regional committees of the Commission should be established in each of the regions identified by the Commission to monitor and inquire into public violence and intimidation. Local and regional security force commanders, and the LDRC and RDRC members, should advise the Commission or a Sub-committee of the Commission of any advance warning of anticipated or current public violence.

6.28   The parties agree that for the Commission to be effective it needs to be a credible instrument. It will furthermore only obtain credibility if it is to be constituted after the National Peace Committee has been consulted. If this condition is met, the establishment of the Commission should be given unconditional support.

6.29   In order to function properly within a legal framework, to exercise the considerable powers given and to obtain State funding, there is no alternative to making use of a statutory enactment, such as the Act. It is suggested that the Act be employed to fulfil this role, because it can be utilised immediately and does not require further statutory attention.

Chapter 7

National Peace Secretariat; Regional and Local Dispute Resolution Committees

7.1   It is clear from the aforegoing that sufficient instruments exist to investigate violence and intimidation and to bring the perpetrators thereof to book. Insufficient instruments exist however to actively combat violence and intimidation at grassroots level. It is therefore proposed that committees be appointed at regional and local levels to assist in this regard. These committees will require national co-ordination.

7.2   In order to provide management skills, budgetary commitment and statutory empowerment and sanction, State involvement is essential.

7.3   A National Peace Secretariat

7.3.1 A National Peace Secretariat shall be established, comprising at least four persons nominated by the National Peace Committee and one representative of the Department of Justice. Further members, up to a maximum of four, may also be appointed.

7.3.2 The function of the National Peace Secretariat will be to establish and co-ordinate Regional Dispute Resolution Committees and thereby Local Dispute Resolution Committees.

7.3.3 The National Peace Secretariat will take decisions on a consensus basis.

7.3.4 The required financial and administrative resources of the National Peace Secretariat, and the other bodies established by it, will be provided by the Department of Justice.

7.4 Regional and Local Dispute Committees

7.4.1 Peace bodies are to be established at both regional and local level, to be styled "Regional Dispute Resolution Committees" (RDRC) and "Local Dispute Resolution Committees" (LDRC) respectively.

7.4.2 Just as the Commission will gain its legitimacy from its composition, reflecting the interested and relevant organisations, the RDRC's and LDRC's will gain their legitimacy by representing the people and communities they are designed to serve.

7.4.3 The areas of jurisdiction of the RDRC's shall be decided by the National Peace Secretariat until such time as statutory provision is made.

7.4.4 RDRC's will be constituted as follows:

7.4.4.1 representatives from relevant political organisations;

7.4.4.2 representatives from relevant churches;

7.4.4.3 representatives of relevant trade unions, industry and business in the region;

7.4.4.4 representatives of relevant local and tribal authorities; and

7.4.4.5 representatives from the police and the defence force.

7.4.5 Duties of RDRC's shall include the following:

7.4.5.1 attending to any matter referred to it by the LDRC, the National Peace Secretariat or the Commission;

7.4.5.2 advising the Commission on matters causing violence and intimidation in its region;

7.4.5.3 settling disputes causing public violence or intimidation by negotiating with the parties concerned and recording the terms of such settlements;

7.4.5.4 guiding LDRC's in their duties;

7.4.5.5 monitoring current applicable peace accords and future peace agreements entered into in the relevant region and settling disputes arising from them;

7.4.5.6 informing the National Peace Secretariat of steps taken to prevent violence and intimidation in its region including breaches of Peace Agreements; and

7.4.5.7 consulting with relevant authorities in its region to combat or prevent violence and intimidation.

7.4.6   The communities within which LDRC's are to be established should be identified by the RDRC's.

7.4.7   LDRC's will be constituted by drawing representatives reflecting the needs of the relevant community.

7.4.8   Duties of the LDRC's shall include the following:

7.4.8.1 attending to any matter referred to it by either the Commission or the RDRC's;

7.4.8.2 creating trust and reconciliation between grassroots community leadership of relevant organisations, including the police and the defence force;

7.4.8.3 co-operating with the local Justice of the Peace in combating and preventing violence and intimidation;

7.3.8.4 settling disputes causing public violence or intimidation by negotiating with the parties concerned and recording the terms of such settlements;

7.4.8.5 eliminating conditions which may harm peace accords or peaceful relations;

7.4.8.6 reporting and making recommendations to the relevant RDRC's;

7.4.8.7 to promote compliance with currently valid and future peace accords and agreements entered into in the relevant area;

7.4.8.8 to agree upon rules and conditions relating to marches, rallies and gatherings; and

7.4.8.9 liaise with local police and local magistrates on matters concerning the prevention of violence, the holding of rallies, marches
and gatherings.

7.5   Justices of the Peace

7.5.1   It is proposed that additional Justices of the Peace be appointed
after consultation with the relevant parties and the LDRC's. The
purpose of the Justices of the Peace will essentially be to promote the peace process at grassroots level and to assist the
LDRC's in their activities.

7.5.2   Duties of Justices of the Peace shall include the following:

7.5.2.1 investigating any complaint received from anyone pertaining to
public violence and intimidation, except where legal processes or
investigations instituted by the South African Police, other police
forces, the Commission, the RDRC's, the Police Reporting Officer
or a commission of inquiry are dealing with the relevant matter;

7.5.2.2 mediating between relevant parties to a dispute by negotiation;

7.5.2.3 applying rules of natural justice when issuing an order which
will be fair and just in the particular circumstances in order to
restore peaceful relations;

7.5.2.4 referring facts constituting an offence to the relevant Attorney-
General;

7.5.2.5 in co-operation with parties and in consultation with the LDRC's
acting as the ears and eyes of LDRC's and reacting in urgent cases;

7.5.2.6 in all matters relating to public violence reporting to the LDRC;
and

7.5.2.7 to pronounce as a judgment the terms of a settlement reached at
LDRC's or RDRC's, provided that the terms of such settlement
are executable.

7.6   RDRC's, LDRC's and Justices of the Peace shall be empowered to:

7.6.1   request the presence of any person with knowledge of any acts
of violence or intimidation to give evidence;

7.6.2   request that any person in possession of any relevant document or other evidentiary material put the same at their disposal; and

7.6.3   protect the identity and safety of anyone assisting the relevant body as contemplated in 7.6.1 and 7.6.2 by excluding the public and/or media from its proceedings or by limiting access to its documents or reports or by prohibiting the publication of the contents of any of its documents or reports.

7.7   The National Peace Secretariat shall assist RDRC's in the exercise of their duties.

7.8   RDRC's may limit the number of members of a LDRC taking into account the prevailing circumstances in the community.

7.9   RDRC's shall determine the boundaries of the area constituting the jurisdiction of LDRC's within their own areas of jurisdiction.

7.10   The National Peace Secretariat and the Commission will advise on the policy to be applied to and by the RDRC's and the LDRC's and the management of the said bodies.

7.11   Members of the RDRC's, LDRC's and Justices of the Peace not in the full-time employment of the State shall be entitled to remuneration and allowances to be paid by the State.

7.12   RDRC's and LDRC's shall appoint chairmen and vice-chairmen to represent the RDRC or LDRC concerned for a period of one year.

7.13   RDRC's and LDRC's shall furnish the National Peace Secretariat, the Commission or the relevant RDRC, as the case may be, with any information required by such bodies.

7.14   In view of the lack of effective peace promoting mechanisms at grassroots level it is urgent that these proposals be implemented as soon as possible. Because of the said urgency, it is agreed that the proposals be implemented on a voluntary basis at the outset. In order to give permanency and effectivity to the proposed structures it will have to be given statutory recognition as soon as possible. This should also ensure that the structures be funded by the State. In drafting the required legislation there should be wide consultation including with the National Peace Committee.

The proposed legislation will also be published for general information and comment.

7.15   In order to ensure the proper functioning of the LDRC's, it is necessary to:

7.15.1 give them high status in their communities for their role in the peace process;

7.15.2 compensate the members of LDRC's for out-of-pocket expenses for attending meetings; and

7.15.3 train the members of the LDRC's in conciliating disputes, running meetings, negotiating skills, etc.

Chapter 8

National Peace Committee

8.1   Composition

8.1.1   Those political parties and organisations currently represented on the Preparatory Committee shall constitute the National Peace Committee together with representatives drawn from other signatory parties where the National Peace Committee believes such inclusion will give effect to the National Peace Accord.

8.1.2   The National Peace Committee shall appoint a chairperson and vice-chairperson, who shall be drawn from the religious and business communities.

8.2   Objective

The objective of the National Peace Committee is to monitor and to make recommendation on the implementation of the National Peace Accord as a whole and to ensure compliance with the Code of Conduct for Political Parties and Organisations.

8.3   Functions

8.3.1   The functions of the National Peace Committee shall be *inter alia* to:

8.3.1.1 perform those functions imposed upon it by the National Peace Accord;

8.3.1.2 receive and consider reports by the National Peace Secretariat and the Commission;

8.3.1.3 decide disputes concerning the interpretation of the Code of Conduct for Political Parties and Organisations;

8.3.1.4 resolve disputes concerning alleged transgressions of the Code of Conduct for Political Parties and Organisations;

8.3.1.5 convene a meeting of the signatories in the event of an unresolved breach of the National Peace Accord; and

8.3.1.6 recommend legislation to give effect to the National Peace Accord.

8.4 Powers

8.4.1 The National Peace Committee shall have the following powers:

8.4.1.1 promote the aims and spirit of the National Peace Accord;

8.4.1.2 convene a meeting of the signatories where necessary;

8.4.1.3 amend the constitution of the National Peace Committee;

8.4.1.4 negotiate and conclude further agreements to achieve the objects of the National Peace Accord.

8.5 Meetings

8.5.1 The National Peace Committee shall elect a chairperson who shall not be a representative of any of the signatory parties.

8.5.2 Meetings shall take place on a regular basis at a date and time agreed to in advance.

8.5.3 Urgent meetings shall be convened by the chairperson on not less than 48 hours' notice in writing to the authorised representatives.

8.5.4 The service of written notice of a meeting at the specified address of the authorised person shall constitute due notice.

8.5.5 An urgent meeting shall be called by the chairperson on a written request of one of the signatory parties to the National Peace Accord.

8.6   Voting

8.6.1   All decisions shall be by consensus.

8.6.2   In the event of a dispute over the interpretation of the National Peace Accord, the failure of the National Peace Committee to achieve consensus at the meeting at which the dispute is raised or at such further meetings as agreed, the dispute shall be referred to expedited arbitration in the manner set out in paragraph 9.4.

8.6.3   In the event of a breach of the National Peace Accord not being resolved by consensus at a meeting of the National Peace Committee, the chairperson of the National Peace Committee shall convene a meeting of national leadership of the signatories within 30 days of that meeting.

Chapter 9

Enforcing the Peace Agreement Between the Parties

9.1   There should be simple and expeditious procedures for the resolution of disputes regarding transgressions of the Code of Conduct for Political Parties and Organisations by political parties and organisations who are signatories of the National Peace Accord. These disputes should wherever possible, be settled:

9.1.1   at grassroots level;

9.1.2   through the participation of the parties themselves; and

9.1.3   by using the proven methods of mediation, arbitration and adjudication.

9.2   Disputes and complaints regarding the transgression of the Code of Conduct for Political Parties and Organisations shall be referred to the National Peace Committee or a committee to whom it has referred the matter for resolution, if the parties were not able to resolve the dispute themselves.

9.3   Where the dispute cannot be resolved by the National Peace
         Committee or the committee to whom it has been referred to by
         the National Peace Committee, it shall be referred for arbitration.

9.4   The arbitrator shall be a person with legal skills, appointed by
         the relevant parties by consensus, failing which the arbitrator
         shall be appointed by the National Peace Committee within 21
         days of being requested to do so in writing and failing which the
         Chairperson of the National Peace Committee shall appoint an
         arbitrator.

9.5   Subject to the above, the procedure of the arbitration shall be as
         follows:

9.5.1   the complaint shall be referred to the arbitrator by the com-
         plaining parties;

9.5.2   the arbitrator shall decide on a date of hearing and call upon
         the parties to the dispute to be present at the hearing with their
         witnesses;

9.5.3   the hearing shall be conducted in private;

9.5.4   the arbitrator shall make a finding on the facts and make an
         order on the organisation concerned to remedy the breach either
         by a public distancing of the organisation from the events or by
         steps to be taken to prevent further breaches of the Code and
         the time within which the order has to be implemented;

9.5.5   the arbitrator shall hold a compliance hearing once the time
         period has expired to determine compliance;

9.5.6   the arbitrator will then submit a report of its findings to the
         National Peace Committee.

9.6   The signatories agree to consult each other in the National Peace
         Committee on methods of ensuring that the Code of Conduct
         for Political Parties and Organisations is enforceable on all such
         bodies, including the possibility of statutory enforcement.

Chapter 10

Special Criminal Courts

10.1 An effective and credible criminal judicial system requires the swift but just dispensation of justice. This in turn will promote the restoration of peace and prosperity to communities, freeing them of the ravages of violence and intimidation. Special attention should be given to unrest related cases, cases of public violence and cases involving intimidation by setting up Special Criminal Courts specifically for the purpose.

10.2 It is agreed that the Department of Justice, in co-operation with local legal practitioners of the Law Societies and the Bar, should establish project committees to advise the Department of Justice on the administration of the proposed Special Criminal Courts.

10.3 These Special Criminal Courts will not deal with ordinary day-to-day crime. Its function will be to deal with unrest related cases. As a result, cases being heard in these courts will be disposed of swiftly and effectively without delay. Cognizance is taken of the initiative to establish mobile courts in certain areas to bring justice closer to the people. The initiative is supported.

10.4 Special Criminal Courts should be located in areas where its services are most urgently needed. This implies that cases can be heard more expeditiously than ordinary criminal courts would be able to. This ensures that perpetrators of violence and intimidation will not unnecessarily be let out on bail enabling them to become re-involved in violence and intimidation. This also ensures that those who are maliciously accused of being violent can have their names cleared sooner than is the case at present.

10.5 The Criminal Law Amendment Act of 1991 provides a mechanism for a programme of witness protection. It is based on the voluntary co-operation of the person threatened by others and can also protect his family members. It is agreed that these provisions be actively utilised in areas affected by unrest.

10.6 For unrest, political violence and intimidation related offences to be effectively combated, criminals should be prosecuted as effectively as possible and at the earliest instance.

10.7   It is acknowledged that for Special Criminal Courts to be effec-
        tive, special procedural and evidential rules should apply. The
        parties therefore commit themselves to promoting procedural
        and evidential rules that will facilitate the expeditious and effec-
        tive hearing of criminal cases.

INDEX

United States Institute of Peace

The United States Institute of Peace is an independent, nonpartisan federal institution created and funded by Congress to strengthen the nation's capacity to promote the peaceful resolution of international conflict. Established in 1984, the Institute meets its congressional mandate through an array of programs, including grants, fellowships, conferences and workshops, library services, publications, and other educational activities. The Institute's Board of Directors is appointed by the President of the United States and confirmed by the Senate.

Board of Directors

Chester A. Crocker (Chairman), Distinguished Research Professor of Diplomacy, School of Foreign Service, Georgetown University

Max M. Kampelman, Esq. (Vice Chairman), Fried, Frank, Harris, Shriver and Jacobson, Washington, D.C.

Dennis L. Bark, Senior Fellow, Hoover Institution on War, Revolution and Peace, Stanford University

Thomas E. Harvey, former general counsel, United States Information Agency

Theodore M. Hesburgh, President Emeritus, University of Notre Dame

William R. Kintner, Professor Emeritus of Political Science, University of Pennsylvania

Christopher H. Phillips, former U.S. ambassador to Brunei

Elspeth Davies Rostow, Stiles Professor of American Studies Emerita, Lyndon B. Johnson School of Public Affairs, University of Texas

Mary Louise Smith, civic activist; former chairman, Republican National Committee

W. Scott Thompson, Professor of International Politics, Fletcher School of Law and Diplomacy, Tufts University

Allen Weinstein, President, Center for Democracy, Washington, D.C.

Members ex officio

Ralph Earle II, Deputy Director, U.S. Arms Control and Disarmament Agency

Toby Trister Gati, Assistant Secretary of State for Intelligence and Research

Ervin J. Rokke, Lieutenant General, U.S. Air Force; President, National Defense University

Walter B. Slocombe, Under Secretary of Defense for Policy

Richard H. Solomon, President, United States Institute of Peace (nonvoting)

Jennings Randolph Program for International Peace

As part of the statute establishing the United States Institute of Peace, Congress envisioned a fellowship program that would appoint "scholars and leaders of peace from the United States and abroad to pursue scholarly inquiry and other appropriate forms of communication on international peace and conflict resolution." The program was named after Senator Jennings Randolph of West Virginia, whose efforts over four decades helped to establish the Institute.

Since it began in 1987, the Jennings Randolph Program has played a key role in the Institute's effort to build a national center of research, dialogue, and education on critical problems of conflict and peace. Through a rigorous annual competition, outstanding men and women from diverse nations and fields are selected to carry out projects designed to expand and disseminate knowledge on violent international conflict and the wide range of ways it can be peacefully managed or resolved.

The Institute's Distinguished Fellows and Peace Fellows are individuals from a wide variety of academic and other professional backgrounds who work at the Institute on research and education projects they have proposed and participate in the Institute's collegial and public outreach activities. The Institute's Peace Scholars are doctoral candidates at American universities who are working on their dissertations.

Institute fellows and scholars have worked on such varied subjects as international negotiation, regional security arrangements, conflict resolution techniques, international legal systems, ethnic and religious conflict, arms control, and the protection of human rights, and these issues have been examined in settings throughout the world.

As part of its effort to disseminate original and useful analyses of peace and conflict to policymakers and the public, the Institute publishes book manuscripts and other written products that result from the fellowship work and meet the Institute's high standards of quality.

Joseph Klaits
Director